WHERE SHALL I LIVE WHEN I RETIRE?

A resource for singles and couples planning next step of their lives or assisting family members in finding care facilities

Carol A. King

Route To Retirement

Copyright ©2017 Carol A. King

All Rights Reserved.

ISBN 978-0-692-04701-9

Acknowledgements

I would like to acknowledge and thank the many people who have contributed to this book and supported me in its development. I would like to thank Jessica Fogg, Vice President of Sales & Marketing with Lutheran Social Ministries of New Jersey, for her encouragement and in-depth review of the independent housing and CCRC sections.

John George, PhD, my colleague in the Next Step Program at the Princeton Senior Resource Center. John's critique of the draft of this book was most helpful, and his friendship is invaluable.

Soni Pahadi, Aging Life Care Professional (Geriatric Care Manager) at Aging Advisors LLC.

Peter Dykes, Sales and Marketing Counselor, Princeton Windrows, Princeton NJ.

Many of my friends have read a draft of this book, and gave me valuable feedback: Celia Lidz, who found the typos, also Toby Adler, Joan Cutler, Carol Dwyer, Debra Lambo, Marlene Lucchesi, Ralph Perry, Valerie Rose, Kim Vu, and Judy Weinberg. Thank you all!

Most of all I would like to thank the people who have attended my presentations and groups, and shared their stories of their retirement journeys. They enriched the lives of other attendees; they also enriched my own life and personal journey.

Table of Contents

Prologue	1
Chapter 1: Introduction	3
Family	7
Chapter 2: Housing Costs & Financing	9
Rent vs. buy	11
Should I take out a mortgage?	13
Interim financing	14
Reverse mortgage	16
Affordable and subsidized housing	17
Other options to help with housing costs	18
Chapter 3: Aging in Place	21
Planning for disasters	31
Home renovation	32
Technology	38
Chapter 4: Relocating	40
Some of the rating scales	43
Living overseas	45
Second home	49
Chapter 5: Downsizing and Moving	50
Stuff (2011)	50
Chapter 6: Housing Options for the Go-Go years	57
55 plus or age-restricted communities	57
Alternatives to independent senior housing	59
I don't wanna live with a bunch of old people	62

Continuing care retirement communities (CCRCs)	64
CCRC contracts	69
Refundable entrance fees	72
Chapter 7: Slow-Go and No-Go Years	**73**
Home services and home health care	75
Types of care in the home	76
Geriatric care managers	78
Hiring a home care or home health care aide	79
Hiring through an agency	81
Chapter 8: Care Facilities - Assisted Living and Nursing Homes	**83**
How likely is it that I will need care?	84
Controlling the decision	86
Assisted living	86
Residential care homes and adult foster care homes	88
Nursing homes	88
Paying for nursing home care	90
Green House Project	91
Memory care units for dementia and Alzheimer's patients	92
Chapter 9: Conclusion	**93**
About the Author	94
Resources	96
Books	96
Links listed in this book	96
Other helpful websites	101

Prologue

In the retirement workshops and programs that I run, the question: "Where shall we live when we retire?" comes up frequently. Housing decisions have probably the most far-reaching impact on your life satisfaction and well-being in retirement. I have identified five big questions to be considered:

- Geography – what locations are you considering? Seashore? Mountains? Urban? Rural? What kind of climate are you looking for?
- Sociology – where are your friends, family, social networks, activities? A social support network is one of the most valuable assets you can have.
- Psychology – feelings about your home and home ownership. Is your home part of your personal identity? Are home-based activities such as gardening what give meaning to your life?
- Physiology – preparing for aging. How will you live in your home as you age? What design features should you be seeking?
- Financial – housing expenses will probably be your biggest cash outlay going forward, and that can greatly impact your lifestyle. What can you afford?

We will be examining these issues in the coming pages. While this book is written for Boomers planning their own retirement living, there is information here that will be helpful for people with aging parents or other family members with care needs. We don't pick a nursing home for ourselves when we are active and vital, but many Boomers are having to deal with these issues for their parents or other family members.

I have also tried to include options for people of various income levels. Unfortunately, the availability of housing for low-income people is limited, and there are long waiting lists for affordable and subsidized housing in many areas.

This book has many links to resources on the Internet. Links do change or become broken over time. I have put all these links on my website and will try to keep them up to date. https://route2retirement.com/resources. Please let me know if you find a broken link. You can email me at Carol.King@route2retirement.com. Thank you.

Chapter 1: Introduction

Richard Leider[1], in his book *Repacking Your Bags: Lighten Your Load for the Good Life*, defines the Good Life as:
>Living in the place you belong
>With the people you love
>Doing the right work
>On Purpose

He puts the place piece first: it provides a space and community to support your work (meaningful activity – paid or unpaid) and your relationships, and space where you can find meaning or purpose in your life.

When I started to do some research on the topic of retirement housing, I found two types of literature. The first category is all about the geography of the destination – *Worst States for Retirement*, *Top Metropolitan Areas for Retirement*, etc. These cover what I call the externals – what does a specific place have to offer, or not offer in the case of negative reports.

The second group of literature was about where to put mom or dad -- finding a living situation for an aging parent or relative who needs some level of care. Neither of these types of material deal with the psychological aspects and meaning of home and how they change as we age. Stephen M. Golant, in his excellent book *Aging in the Right Place*, uses the term *residential normalcy*:

---

[1] Leider, Richard. *Repacking Your bags: Lighten Your Load for the Good Life.* Berrett-Koehler Publishers, Inc. 2012.

When people find their right place to live, they have achieved *residential normalcy*. This happens in the place where they experience overall pleasurable, hassle-free and memorable feelings that have relevance to them; and where they feel both competent and in control – that is, they do not have to behave in personally objectionable ways or to unduly surrender mastery of their lives or environments to others[2].

You probably will make several moves after you retire. While most people tend to stay in their own communities when they retire, preferably in their current homes, some will move to more suitable housing in the same community. Others will opt to relocate to areas with warmer climates, lower taxes and living costs, and amenities that they value. Florida and the southwest have been the favored locations until recently. Then, as they age, or as their spouses die, they move closer to an adult child. Even in multi-tiered senior communities, couples may move into a cottage or villa, and when one partner dies, the surviving spouse may move into a condominium within the community. If it is a continuing care retirement community (CCRC), the move may be from independent living (cottage or condominium) to assisted living, and then possibly to a nursing care unit.

---

[2] Golant, Stephen. *Aging in the Right Place*, Health Professions Press, Inc. 2015. viii.

The fact is: you will need different types of housing and services as you age. Retirement has been described as a sequence – the go-go years, the slow-go years, and the no-go years. Ideally, your plan for retirement will be comprehensive, considering what your housing needs will be at each stage of the sequence. Housing that is appropriate for a couple in the go-go years could be totally inadequate for a single person in the no-go years. At that point, you may be forced to make a move that will be much more wrenching than if you had planned for those needs up front. Also, the older one is when making a move, the more difficult the adjustment. For a frail older person, a move can hasten his or her decline dramatically.

There are many things in retirement that we can't control, but we can control where we live – up to a point. There may come a time when you are unable to make that decision and others will make it for you. You need to make your own choices while you are still able; if you don't, the time will come when someone else will make them for you – an adult child, guardian, or even the courts. Your options at that point will probably be much more limited. You might not like any of the choices made for you, but you will have no choice but to live with them. One man was diagnosed with early stage Alzheimer's disease. On his better days, he had his wife drive him to the various memory care units in their area, and he told her what he liked and did not like about each one. He not only was making his preferences known, he was absolving his wife of the guilt she would no doubt feel when the time came that she had to place him in such a unit.

We may be able and active now, but we never know when a 'crisis event' may occur, one which changes everything – heart attack, a fall and a broken hip, a stroke, a car accident, or an Alzheimer's diagnosis. As Diane Twohy Masson[3] put it, "Every senior is one fall away from a crisis." Therefore, having thought through one's housing options for the long term is essential. After a crisis event occurs, you will have very few options, and little or no time to adjust.

While you may not be able to make these decisions after a crisis, (one normally does not pick a nursing home ahead of time unless it is part of a CCRC), you can and should designate a health proxy, and let that person know what your preferences are for long-term care and end of life. A trusted relative or friend can see that your best interests are followed.

Retirement choices are both a financial and a lifestyle matter. These issues are most closely related when it comes to housing – where you live may be driven by what you can afford. The choice is to get the best mix of services and amenities for your money at each stage of life.

Most people want to age in their current home, but this may not be the right place as you age, no matter how many alterations you make to the property. Jon Pynoos, professor of gerontology policy and planning at University of Southern California, uses the term "Peter Pan" housing. He says that most existing homes were built for people who will never grow old. They have stairs, slippery inaccessible bathrooms, narrow halls, galley kitchens, inade-

---

[3] Masson, Diane Twohy. *Your Senior Housing Options.* CreateSpace Independent Publishing Platform. 2015

quate lighting, and lack safeguards to prevent falls. In my area, a lot of split-level houses were built in the 1950s and 1960s, and they are the worst option for senior housing, with steps to get to every level in the house. Furthermore, most housing built in the last 60 years is in the suburbs, and largely inaccessible except by car, leaving residents who don't drive isolated.

Family

For most of us, family is the bedrock of our lives. Family members will no doubt want to have a say in your plans for your retirement, and they may have some valuable advice. Just remember – it is **YOUR** life, not theirs. One issue that may arise is family get-togethers and reunions. These events may be part of the family tradition. But, cooking that Thanksgiving dinner for 25 people will at some point become too much for mom, and something must give. It helps to sit down and have a clear-eyed discussion not just about Thanksgiving, but about family expectations for all the traditional activities.

For couples, it is essential that they agree about their needs in all aspects of retirement, not just housing. If they cannot agree, they need to develop a plan to accommodate each partner's desires. I am amazed at the studies that appear from time to time about how many couples have not even talked about their life plans for retirement, let alone come to an agreement.

Some people, instead of trading down to a smaller house when they became tired of home maintenance efforts, bought bigger houses. A study by AgeWave[4] for Merrill Lynch found that of the retirees who had moved, 50% moved to a smaller home and 30% to a larger home. The rationale is that they wanted to have room for family to visit. I hope that their expectations of family visits panned out. As our children and grandchildren grow older, they have their own lives and plans. It becomes harder and harder (not to mention perhaps more expensive) to plan a trip to see grandma and grandpa. It is important to have everyone on the same page. Adult children may not want to spend their vacations at their parents' homes. Instead of maintaining a big house for those occasional visitors, it may pay to set up a family reunion at a centrally located resort where nobody needs to do any cooking or cleaning, and everyone can enjoy each other's company. Or perhaps one of your adult children may be very happy to take over the role of family host. You won't know unless you ask. Another reason for retirees buying a larger house was the desire for a newer, updated home with more amenities and space for the hobbies or home office. Hopefully, these home buyers have sufficient financial resources to maintain a bigger house.

---

[4] *Home in Retirement: More Freedom, New Choices.* AgeWave for Merrill Lynch. 2015.

Chapter 2: Housing Costs & Financing

Before one retires, the financial focus is on saving and investing for retirement. After retirement, that focus shifts from building up the saving and investment portfolio to managing cash flow and preserving assets. Housing is a big part of that picture. Some pre-retirees consider their home as the basis for funding their retirement and assume they will downsize to supplement their cash flow in retirement. But, even if you own your house outright, you have an investment in an illiquid asset – you can't take bricks and mortar to the grocery store. If you still have a mortgage when you retire, those mortgage payments may be a big part of your cash outlay each month, along with utility bills, real estate taxes, maintenance and home owner insurance. You may wind up house-rich and cash-poor. For some home owners, those ongoing housing costs are the motivation to downsize and move to a smaller home. For renters, the costs are much simpler and predictable – rent and utilities. (If you must break a lease to move, there will probably be a penalty.)

Downsizing to save money and recoup some of your investment may or may not be a good idea. There are two issues here:

- First, how will your housing costs in a smaller place compare to your current costs? Whether it is less expensive to rent or to own can vary from place to place, even from neighborhood to neighborhood. You will need to do the comparison on specific properties. If you are considering an active adult community or a CCRC, there will be monthly fees which can be sizeable. One thing that is often missed is *opportunity cost*. That is the amount of return you would have gotten if you had invested your house sale proceeds and rented instead of purchasing a new property. If there is not a significant difference between the costs of living in a downsized property and your current home, it may not pay to move.

- The second issue is how much cash will you net from the sale after all expenses are paid? Your home is only worth what someone else is willing to pay for it, and that will depend to a great degree on what other similar properties in the area ("comps" in real estate lingo) are selling for in the current market, as well as the condition and location of your property. What you will net will be the sum of the selling price less repairs you need to undertake to make the property marketable and what the buyer's inspection shows, less the agent's fee and various charges for permits and fees (closing costs), and less any outstanding mortgage balance and liens against the property. You may have to pay capital gains tax if you have a sizeable capital gain on the sale; in 2017, the exclusion is $500,000 for couples, $250,000 for singles. You need to have records of what you have spent on capital improvements over the years. That adds to the cost basis in figuring out your capital gain. Check with your tax advisor for other requirements.

Then, you will have the cost of the packing and moving, plus the costs associated with the purchase of the new place. That may include painting and upgrades you may wish to make to the new property. After all this, how much will you actually net? In the end, it may not be worth it. The alternative may be to invest the proceeds of the sale and rent the new place, or to stay in your current place if it can be made 'age-friendly' with some renovations. It is about choosing the best alternative for maintaining your desired quality of life. A reverse mortgage, which is discussed below, may provide the cash to do that.

The National Council on Aging has a very good tool to help you figure out how a move would impact your finances. It is an Economic Checkup calculator, and you can access it at

https://calculator.benefitscheckup.org/calculators/move-or-stay-put

If you decide to sell your house and move to a senior living facility or CCRC, there are some professionals who can help with various aspects of moving, buying, or selling real estate or renovating property. Look for a Senior Real Estate Specialist (SRES). These agents have a certification from the National Association of Realtors that enables them to address the needs of home buyers and sellers age 50+. Find one at http://seniorsrealestate.com/

Many senior housing developments can also assist you in selling your house and obtaining interim financing if necessary.

Rent vs. buy

The decision of whether to buy or rent your next home is a difficult one. There are both financial issues and emotional ones. Home ownership is part of the American dream, part of our personal identity as solid, worthy citizens. Nevertheless, renting in retirement may be the better option. Real estate values appreciate over a long period of time, and market fluctuations are the norm. In this stage of life, you may not live in the new property long enough to realize much gain, if any. Some experts in the field have estimated that you need to live in a property at least five years to break even on sales and moving costs, but it all depends on market fluctuations during that time period.

Currently, there are shortages of available rentals in many areas. Rising real estate prices have put owning a home beyond the reach of many people, forcing them into the rental market. This in turn has put pressure on rental rates, forcing renters to pay a higher percentage of their income on rent than in the past. AARP has a financial calculator to help you figure out the annual cost of owning a home, which you can then compare with the rental costs in the area: http://www.aarp.org/money/budgeting-saving/rent_buy_home_calculator/

Renting pros:
- Renting is a short-term option; it is easier to move than if you had to sell a home.
- Maintenance and upkeep are the responsibility of the landlord.
- The up-front investment is limited to a rental deposit.
- Your heirs are not saddled with having to sell property to settle the estate.
- Rents are predictable; no unexpected major outlay for home maintenance.
- You may be eligible for federal or state rental assistance or rebate.

Renting cons:
- Rents can and will increase over time.
- You are at the mercy of the landlord for the upkeep of the property.
- You have no tax deduction for real estate taxes or mortgage interest.
- There is no potential equity growth from increasing the value in the home.
- There may be restrictions on pets, noise, or use of the property. However, service animals must be permitted.
- In multi-unit buildings, noise can be a problem, even if there are noise restrictions.
- Your right to renovate or personalize the property is limited. This may impact your mobility within the unit in the future should you need to use a wheelchair. However, under the Federal Fair Housing Act, a landlord cannot refuse to let you make reasonable modifications at your own expense for a disability. You may have to agree to restore the property to its original condition when you move out.
- If you run out of money later, you do not have any equity in the property to tap with a reverse mortgage. Reverse mortgages are discussed below.

Should I take out a mortgage?

Traditionally, financial planners have advised clients to pay off their mortgage before they retire. However, with low interest rates prevailing, this has changed. According to the Federal Reserve Bank, about 42 percent of households headed by someone age 65 to 74 have home-secured debt. This compares with just 18.5 percent in 1992 and 32 percent in 2004. With historically low mortgage interest rates, mortgage holders have figured that they can earn a better after-tax return on their money if they invest it in securities instead of paying off the mortgage. This may be true over the long term; however, retirement housing may be held for a much shorter time span, leaving some advisors to question this strategy.

With interest rates expected to rise, today's home buyers face a different picture. While some lenders have modified their criteria for loans to accommodate retirees, obtaining a mortgage is much more difficult than it was prior to the real estate market crash in 2008. Lenders face much more stringent regulations, which have made qualifying for a mortgage much more difficult. Potential home buyers are encouraged to start the mortgage process before they retire.

Several other options may be available to you. If you are a veteran or the surviving spouse of a veteran, you may qualify for a VA loan at a rate lower than the going market rate. Some states also have housing benefits for veterans.

The Home Ready Program of Fannie May is designed for credit-worthy low-income home-buyers. For retirees, it may include some income from adult children.

Interim financing

If you plan to finance the purchase of your new home from the sale of your current house, you have several options:
- Delay the purchase of a new home until you have closed on the sale of your current home. This will simplify the cash flow situation, but it can lead to

some upheaval if you can't find the place you want and complete the closing by the time you need to move. Timing is everything.
- Liquidate investments to close on the new home. This may result in large tax consequences if there are capital gains. An alternative is to borrow against your investment portfolio.
- Use interim financing to close on the new home while your present home is on the market. There are two types:
    o Bridge loans. These are short-term loans, typically 6 months, designed to get you through the interim period between buying the new and selling the old home. As there are large variations among lenders, you need to shop around. You may be required to take out a mortgage on your new home from the bridge lender.
    o Home equity line of credit. The collateral is your current home. Some lenders will not issue a home equity loan on a property that is on the market. In that case, you must secure the loan before listing the property.

However, if you choose to finance the transaction, it can be stressful. Even if you have a buyer for your home, the sale may fall through. Also, if you have already closed on your new home, you will have the continuing costs of carrying two properties, plus the loan costs. You need to have sufficient cash flow for this.

Reverse mortgage

Reverse mortgages are a way for homeowners over the age 62 to tap the equity in their home and generate cash for living expenses or renovations. However, they are risky and costly. Reverse mortgages are considered a last resort, because interest rates are high, and the offerings are complex. Consult a financial planner with experience in this area before you apply for a reverse mortgage.

With a regular mortgage, the homeowner pays a monthly amount of interest plus principle on the loan (a declining balance). Equity in the home increases as the loan is paid off. With a reverse mortgage, the lender pays the homeowner, and the balance rises. The loan is paid when the home is eventually sold or when the homeowner fails to live in it for 12 consecutive months. Thus, if mom is living in a nursing home, the heirs cannot hold on to the house in the hope of inheriting it. They have the option of paying off the loan if they want to keep the house in the family. If a couple is living in the house, both must be signers to the reverse-mortgage contract; otherwise the remaining, non-signing spouse may be required to pay off the loan or move out if the signing spouse is not living in the house.

The homeowner still holds title to the property and must pay real estate taxes and insurance, and keep the property in good repair. If these restrictions are not met, the lender may call the loan; that is, they will require repayment and not wait for the property to be sold. If the homeowner cannot repay the loan, the lender can foreclose on the property. Over time, if the value of the home falls, the sale may not be sufficient to pay off the loan, but since reverse mortgages are covered by FHA insurance, lenders will be reimbursed for any shortfall.

Loan payouts may be in the form of monthly cash advances, line of credit advances (used when needed), or an initial lump sum, which may be used to pay off any existing mortgage.

Several factors determine how much you can borrow and the interest rate you pay. The value of the property and amount of equity you have in it are two factors. The third is the age of the borrower. Older borrowers will live in the home for a shorter time than younger people, and therefore will "consume" less of the loan.

A reverse mortgage is a complicated financial instrument. Whether it is right for you will depend on your specific situation. If you decide to go this route, have a real estate lawyer review the loan papers before you sign. Some local senior centers or other nonprofit groups may offer reverse mortgage counseling. The Federal Trade Commission has a good website on reverse mortgages:

https://www.consumer.ftc.gov/articles/0192-reverse-mortgages

Affordable and subsidized housing

Many of the housing options discussed below are unaffordable for many people, and there are far too few low-cost options available. Existing facilities usually have long waiting lists. Depending on the source of funding, some facilities may only be available to local residents. Here are some terms you should know when searching for low-cost housing:

- Market rate – the owner/landlord charges what the market will bear.

- Affordable housing – rates vary based on income and assets levels. Affordable units may be interspersed with market rate units. These may be rentals or condos available for sale. A condo owner can sell the unit, but the buyer must be qualified according to the restrictions in the deed. Congregate housing, described below, is usually affordable housing.
- Subsidized housing – low rents are subsidized by the federal government (HUD).

If you are looking for affordable or subsidized housing, contact your community's housing office, senior center, or the county Agency on Aging for information and application forms.

Other options to help with housing costs
- Benefits checkup. The National Council on Aging has an excellent program called a Benefits Checkup. Based on information that you provide, it will review all benefit programs you may qualify for. Information can be found here: https://www.benefitscheckup.org/ Contact your local senior center or county Agency on Aging if you need assistance using this program.
- Another benefits checkup site is https://www.benefits.gov/
- HUD has a website that links to various local home-buying programs at https://portal.hud.gov/hudportal/HUD?src=/buying/localbuying
- Tax assistance. In some states, real estate taxes may be reduced for older homeowners. In others,

there may be a cap placed on how much real estate taxes can be increased, if any, over a base level. In New Jersey, this is called Senior Freeze. Check with your local and state taxation departments. Also, ask your local tax assessor to review the valuation of your house. You may be able to get it lowered, thus reducing your real estate tax.

- Utility assistance. The Low-Income Home Energy Assistance Program (LIHEAP) is a program of the US Department of Health and Human Services. It helps low income families with heating and cooling costs, home weatherizing and energy-related repairs. Your state and local utility companies may also have programs to help low income homeowners.
- Have your insurance policies reviewed. You may not need the coverage you have been paying for, and your agent may be able to find you an appropriate policy at a lower cost.
- Renting out rooms. You may be able to rent out an unused bedroom to someone in exchange for household chores or for cash. If you live near a college, contact the college's housing office to see if you can list your room there. This can work very well, but you need to be careful about who you let into your house. Check backgrounds thoroughly. Also, get your agreement in writing. LawDepot.com has some good information on rental agreements. https://www.lawdepot.com/contracts/roommate-agreement Rental income is taxable, but you can deduct expenses related to the rental. Check with your tax advisor for details.

- Take in a senior house-mate. Or move in with someone else. A housemate can not only provide some income, but he or she can also provide companionship and security. There are websites that match up potential roommates. Seniorly.com is one of them: https://www.seniorly.com/. Another is Silvernest: https://www.silvernest.com/ As with a room rental, get an agreement on the terms in writing.
- Live with family. Many seniors express the feeling that they do not want to move in with their adult children – they want to maintain their independence and not become a burden, but this is still an option. Some families have dealt with the independence issue by creating a separate apartment for their parents in their home.

Chapter 3: Aging in Place

According to AARP, almost 90% of seniors want to remain in their homes, that is, to age in place. Perhaps you do as well. Let us examine this decision. Is it a default or fallback position? As in 'I just don't want to think about it, so I will stay here?'

Is it because the thought of cleaning out the house and getting rid of years of accumulated stuff is daunting? Or is it the demands of searching for a new place and making all the decisions associated with it – location, suitability, financing, possibly some remodeling, and then facing the physical demands of the actual move, after which there is the task of getting adjusted to a new place, a new neighborhood, doctors and services, and perhaps a new community?

Some seniors place a very high priority on maintaining their independence, and not wanting to live with adult children or other relatives, or in a facility where they would have to live by 'rules' and compromise their independence. For others, their home is a reflection of their identity – their place in the community – a statement that they have lived successful or accomplished lives. Even though they may not be active in the roles they once held, the house that is evidence of past economic or social position is difficult to give up.

Clare Cooper Marcus[5] in her book *House as Mirror of Self* called home a place of self-expression, a refuge from the outside world, a cocoon where we can feel nurtured and let down our guard. Where we live is closely tied up with our psychological development. The house, its setting and its furnishings may help us to become who we are meant to be, or it can smother us. And this can change over time. A house that nurtured us and our growing family can become a millstone when the children are gone, and all that is left is memories, which are hard to give up. A widower friend of mine who is over 90 said, "I don't need a five-bedroom house. I live in the downstairs bedroom, kitchen and family room. But this house has my wife's fingerprints all over it. I can't give that up." Some parents think that their grown children would be bereft if they did not have their old family home to return to for visits. Such attachment to the home is a compelling argument for staying there.

A more serious issue is when a senior refuses to accept the reality of aging and decline; when they state, "I'm OK!" when clearly, they are not. Perhaps the senior does not remember any difficulty, or is afraid of the consequences – the huge adjustment that would be required to make a change, and the loss of control and independence. Perhaps one spouse is worn out with caring for the other spouse but feels it is her duty. Sometimes a couple is able

---

[5] Marcus, Clare Cooper. *House as a Mirror of Self: Exploring the Deeper Meaning of Home.* Nicolas-Hays, Inc. 2nd edition 2006.

to manage because one's abilities offset the other's inabilities. However, when one spouse is gone, the remaining one cannot cope. At this point, an intervention is needed.

This discussion isn't just about denial, being stubborn, or wishful thinking. It is about making mindful choices about what type of housing will work best for you as you age. Stephen Golant sheds some light on this issue with the concept of residential normalcy, as defined earlier. He calls residential normalcy "the sweet spot to live." The resident is in his or her comfort zone and in the mastery zone. That is, having pleasurable feelings and memories about the environment and activities in that place. Mastery means feeling competent and in control in that residential environment.

Golant[6] describes the "push-pull" factors driving older adults' decisions to stay or move. Push factors involve a failure to cope with existing housing problems – that is, the inability to achieve residential normalcy. They must be able to move – and have credible alternatives that they can afford. Thirdly, they must believe that there are feasible alternatives, and that these alternatives will significantly increase their residential comfort and mastery – the pull factor.

So, a person in the residential normalcy sweet spot would not be inclined to relocate, despite what, to an observer, is an undesirable place to live, both now and in the future. The observer is using a different set of criteria than the resident, who may place a much higher priority

---

[6] Golant, 2015. 106.

on the emotional ties and the familiar (knowing where the light switches are, for example); conversely, the observer may only see the external attributes of the home.

So, how do we deal with this issue? First, I have found almost no research on when, in the retirement journey, people make a move. However, personal observation tells me that the older one is, the more difficult it is to make a move. This is borne out to some extent by research done by Professor Jamie Patrick Hopkins, Professor of Retirement Income Planning and Co-Director of the American College New York Life Center for Retirement Income Planning of the American College of Financial Services. In his research, he found that the desire to age in place increases significantly as respondents become older. "We saw more uncertainty between the ages of 55 and 62. But once we started getting past 62 and you start moving into retirement, we saw that these individuals really don't expect or want to leave their homes,[7]" he said. However, they may be forced to confront their declining capability of maintaining a house independently.

---

[7] *Retirees Clear in New Survey: We Want to Stay in Our Homes.* The American College of Financial Services. The American College of Financial Services. May 23, 2016.

In his book Elderburbia[8]: Philip B. Stafford cites research that identifies who among the older population moves, but not necessarily when they move. They were:
- Amenity-seekers, typically healthy, married and financially secure. They seek communities with appealing amenities.
- Assistance-seekers, characterized by greater residential and economic dependence on others, typically family members, for income and housing.
- Individuals relocating in response to the development of a severe disability. They typically are moving to a nursing home or the residence of an adult child.

We can hypothesize though, that the older one is when making the move, the more likely it is that the person has care needs, and that the family is involved in the decision. This kind of move requires a very different decision-making process than that of an active recently retired individual or couple. It may involve the family or advisor dealing with denial or refusal on the part of the elder. It can be very difficult to admit that one's health is failing, that the present living situation is not safe, and that a change must be made.

But let's start with that individual or couple who is in the go-go retirement years. There are many housing alternatives available – an infinite number of options, in your own community and any place else in the country, or

---

[8] Stafford, Philip B. *Elderburbia: Aging with a Sense of Place in America*. Praeger. 2009.

even around the world. The thought boggles the mind! Your current home is only one of those alternatives.

Let's start with the home you have. As we said earlier, you will probably live in several places in retirement. As you age, you may require a different environment, with services you don't need initially. Here is the first question:

How suitable is your present home for your potential needs down the road? **Will this place be the right place for aging in place?** It may be right for the go-go years, but not all that adequate for the slow-go years, and unworkable for the no-go years. As one professional put it "If you want to age in place, you need to be in the right place before you really start to age."

Some people who consider this question jump to the need for renovation – adding a downstairs bathroom with grab bars by the toilet and in the shower. We will talk about home modifications later, but first, let's back up here and consider some even more basic needs than the physical property.

Before you invest in that new bathroom, consider this:

- Research has shown repeatedly that social isolation and loneliness is a major risk factor for functional decline in adults, and is associated with numerous diseases in aging, including dementia. It is not the quantity of relationships, but rather the quality and level of social connection. Individuals can still be lonely even though they may have a spouse and caregivers around.

    The question is: If you can no longer drive or have reduced mobility, can you still easily get to the places where you can meet and socialize with friends? Can you walk there or take public trans-

portation? It is not enough to expect friends to come to visit you. They may not be able to travel either. Also, over time we lose friends – they become disabled, die, or move away. You need to be able to get to places where you can meet new friends and build new relationships. This may be the single most important factor contributing to your wellness and happiness as you age.
- Are there available and easily accessible health care resources near your home? How close and how accessible is the nearest hospital? How comprehensive are the services it offers? How close and accessible are your doctors?
- How near are your family members, and will they be able to give you the time and attention that you may require. What kind of burden would you be placing on them? What are the other options for ongoing care near you?
- Home care. Along with the decision to age in place, is the assumption that home care will be available should it be needed. We will have more to say about home care later, but the first question here is: What resources are available, and how much will they cost? Some seniors have found that the cost of maintaining a home plus paying for home health aides is prohibitive.
- Quality of the community and neighborhood. What is going on in your town? Are taxes rising, or quality of life declining? It makes no sense to invest in a property if the real estate market is declining. Some cities and towns have suffered greatly from loss of employers and jobs, and this

affects the quality of life for everybody. On a smaller scale, what is going on in your neighborhood? Have property values kept pace there? Do you feel safe there? Is there a turnover in the residents moving in and out? Are they the people who will be there for you for the foreseeable future? I am aware of some neighborhoods where everyone was about the same age – they raised their kids together. Now they are all up in years, and nobody can help out their neighbors – they all need help themselves. What about the local shops - are they still there or are they closing or moving away?

Aging in place is also a movement aimed at making communities 'user friendly' for older residents, allowing them to maintain their independence and remain in their own homes. How user-friendly is your community? Here are some factors to consider:

- Availability of community-based aging services delivered to the home. Is there a local network of services you can tap into when you need them? Can an ambulance or emergency crew get to you on a stormy night? Not just health care, but also home maintenance services. Shoveling snow and mowing lawns can get harder every year. You are going to need help with that sooner or later.
- Safe walk-ability to local services: Are there level sidewalks, curb cuts, street crossings, and traffic lights where you need to go? Do you need to cross busy streets?
- Accessible transportation, including bus shelters, and accommodation of mobility devices such as walkers. This includes not only public transit, but

also programs such as para-transit, dial-a-ride, or ride sharing services. Can you get to places where you can engage in meaningful and useful activities – take courses, enjoy music, theater or sporting events, places of worship, the barber shop, doctors' offices, outdoor areas, walking trails, and parks? Can you get to the airport easily when you wish to visit the grandchildren?

- Zoning that permits home renovation, allowing older adults to remain in their homes.
- What is the condition of the house itself? Is there a lot of 'deferred maintenance'? If the house needs a new roof or furnace, or if the windowsills are rotted or the foundation is crumbling, it makes no sense to put more money into a new bathroom. Could you afford the needed major repairs down the line? Remember, you could be paying for home health aides by then. If you live in a multi-unit building or you rent your house, some of the same considerations apply. How well does the landlord maintain the property, and what can you expect in rent increases in the future? Also, what kinds of neighbors do you have? Who is the landlord renting to?

If you are a couple, you are probably sharing the tasks involved with the upkeep of your home. At some point, there will be one person living in the house. Will it be suitable for a single person, or will it be too much work to keep it up alone? What about all the extra space that you will be paying to maintain, - utilities, insurance, and taxes?

Stephen Golant [9] says that that those with the best chances to remain in their current dwellings will have the following advantages going for them:
- The dwelling can be physically retrofitted, redesigned, and equipped with smart home technologies.
- They will have at least one family member or devoted caregiver to assist full-time. They will either live with them, or be close by and be available whenever needed to provide care.
- They will live in a place where they can afford a growing range of home- and community-based care services to help them manage their chronic health problems or their mobility limitations.
- They will occupy "age-friendly" or "healthy-aging" buildings, neighborhoods, or communities that offer older residents a variety of infrastructure and services designed to make it easier for them to age in place.

There is a lot to consider when making the decision to age in place. You may still decide to stay at your current home, or you may decide to move to a different, more suitable place nearby where you can 'age in place.' According to AARP, 38% of older adults moved to new homes for their slow-go and no-go years, but they still aimed to maintain their independence in those new homes. By staying in or near their home community, they maintain their social network – those very important friendships that

---

[9] Golant 2015, p. 62.

mean so much to us. So, aging in place may still involve a move, but the new place will be one where you can successfully navigate as you age. Furthermore, when you make that move early, you have plenty of time to think it through, find the right place, and make that adjustment while you are still physically able to do so.

Planning for disasters

At the time of this writing, images of Hurricane Harvey's flooding in Texas are in the news, along with photos of nursing home residents awaiting rescue while sitting in wheelchairs in water up to their waists. Other photos show able-bodied people being rescued from rooftops and car roofs. How did the home-bound older people make it through? We don't know, but we hope they were able to evacuate. If you are planning to age in place, what is your emergency plan? In an article from Grantmakers in Aging, Jennifer Campbell lists five reasons why more older people die in major disasters: [10]

- They are unable to evacuate quickly due to functional limitations.
- They are slow or reluctant to evacuate. Home is where they feel safe.
- They survived previous disasters and think they will get through the next one.

---

[10] Grantmakers in Aging. https://www.giaging.org/issues/disasters/ 2014.

- They have a chronic condition that deteriorated due to lack of medication or functioning medical equipment.
- They were cut off from help, living in high-rise apartments and isolated areas.

If you decide to age in place, what is your disaster plan?

Home renovation

A report from Harvard University[11] found that, although the market share of homeowners over 55 in the remodeling market increased from 30 percent to 47 percent between 2005 and 2013, increasing accessibility was not a major factor. Instead, these remodelers were looking to increase home value, repair or replace broken or worn-out components or improve energy efficiency. Perhaps they were more focused on preparing the home for eventual sale than living in it themselves. However, the same report found that the majority of occupied housing units in the US are not currently equipped to accommodate disability needs. This was especially true of older homes than those more recently built, which are more inclined to be one story and have open space on the main floor. Yet, of households headed by persons aged 75-84, 50% needed some adjustments, as did 69% of those over the age of 85. The most common areas that required adjustments were the bathrooms and master bedrooms on the first floor; other adjustments included ensuring there were no steps be-

---

[11] *Aging in Place: Implications for Remodeling 2015.* Joint Center for Housing Studies, Harvard University

tween rooms and making bathrooms wheel chair accessible.

You have decided that your current (or new) home is the right place to age in place. Before you jump to calling bathroom contractors, let's talk about making a plan. It makes no sense to add a bathroom if the kitchen is too small to accommodate a wheelchair. By evaluating the whole layout of the house, you may conclude that it is not the best place after all.

Some people fall into what may be called 'incrementalism' – making little adjustments here and there, without having an overall plan – they raise the toilet seat, get rid of the throw rugs, maybe replace a few door knobs with levers, or add some extra lighting as the need arises. Little by little, they are spending more and more money, and still may not have a workable house for the long term.

What are we planning for? Well, to rephrase the question, how does aging affect our needs in a home? Reduced mobility and the need to navigate with walkers and wheel chairs immediately comes to mind, but there are other factors as well. Fall prevention is a major one; some people who fall and end up in the hospital never get to go home at all. Later in the book, we talk about activities of daily living (ADL) and instrumental activities of daily living (IADL) which also have implications for our housing needs as we age.

Aging brings about decline in:
    Hearing
    Vision
    Sense of smell
    Sense of touch and dexterity
    Mobility and agility

Balance and range of motion
Cognition

The Center for Universal Design at North Carolina State University has some resources on their website, including a very good article: *Home Modifications and Products for Safety and Ease of Use*.[12] The authors deal with activities in the home that are affected by a decline in these areas; I will only deal with those that would need to be addressed in a home renovation. Other strategies they mention can be retrofitted as needed. Note that aging is not the only cause of reduced ability. Change can occur at any time of life, and many of these features, such as grab bars, can benefit people of any age or ability level.

- Hearing
    - Install insulating materials to reduce ambient noise, and select appliances such as dishwashers and washing machines that are rated for quietness.
    - Install strobe-light smoke detectors.
- Vision
    - Select appliances and thermostats that have easy to read clocks, dials, and controls.
    - Reduce glare from highly polished surfaces and windows.

---

[12] https://projects.ncsu.edu/ncsu/design/cud/pubs_p/docs/Home%20Modifications%20and%20Products.pdf

- - Provide better, but not glaring lighting, especially task lighting and on stairs. Sky lights work well.
  - Use backlit light switches that glow in the dark, also motion sensor light switches and night lights.
  - Use distinct colors to differentiate different areas of the house, counter tops, and floors.
- Smell
  - Select smoke and carbon monoxide (which is odorless) detectors that have both visual and aural signals.
- Touch and dexterity
  - Use levered handles for door knobs and faucets; C-or D-shaped loop handles on cabinet doors and drawers.
  - Electrical controls, outlets, and thermostats must be accessible. Use rocker panels or touch pads for light switches and push-button combination locks.
- Strength and range of motion (includes wheelchair users)
  - Reduce barriers inside and outside of the home. Eliminate steps and changes in floor level. Ensure the bedroom, bathroom, and laundry are on the first floor.
  - For a fully accessible bathroom, install a curb-less shower with seat, flexible hose and hand-held shower head, and anti-scald valves. The lavatory should have recessed space below for knees and wheelchair. The

toilet should be 'comfort height,' 19 inches above the floor.
- In the kitchen, select pull-out cutting boards, base cabinets with pull-out drawers and revolving corner storage, recessed space below a work surface, ovens that are accessible from a seated height, and a near-by landing space. Some manufacturers make wall cabinets that can be pulled down to be accessible to someone seated.
- Select hard flooring, high-density low-pile carpeting, and non-slip tiles for the kitchen and bathroom.
- Install grab bars in reinforced walls in the shower or toilet area. In other areas, install hand rails. Grab bars and hand rails can be retrofitted, but must be firmly attached to a reinforced wall (a stud).
- Halls and passage ways need to be at least 32 inches wide with a straight approach; 36 inches with a turning space. Doors should be 36" wide, since the edge of an open door will reduce the width of the opening. If the entry cannot accommodate a 36" door, a pocket door may be the solution, or simply remove the door if privacy is not an issue.
- A wheelchair requires at least 60 inches to make a 180-degree turn. Turning space must be provided at entry ways and at corners in hallways. Also, if you install a stair lift, provide turning space at the top and bottom of the stairs.

- Outdoors, eliminate long, crooked or inclined pathways; if there is a step at the entrance, install a ramp. The guideline is one foot of ramp for each inch rise.
- Throughout the house, provide accessible storage space for items close to the spot where they are used.
- Balance and coordination
  - Install a comfort height toilet.
  - Eliminate throw and scatter rugs, and secure area rugs.
  - Install handrails and supports.
  - Enhance vision.
- Cognition
  - Install safety-designed appliances; cooktops that show red when hot (even if turned off).

Sometimes home modification is needed after a health crisis, while the older person is living in the house. This can produce resistance for fear of disruption, and making the home look more 'institutionalized.' There are many ways this can be avoided. The National Association of Home Builders has a program called CAPS – Certified Aging in Place Specialists. You can find local CAPS-certified builders in your state at http://www.nahb.org/en/find/directory-designee.aspx. NAHB also has a checklist for aging in place renovations at http://www.nahb.org/en/learn/designations/certified-aging-in-place-specialist/related-resources/aging-in-place-remodeling-checklist.aspx

Another good resource is the Aging in Place website http://ageinplace.com

The web site eldercare.gov has a number of resources on home modification, including a checklist for hiring a contractor and sources for financing.
http://eldercare.gov/Eldercare.NET/Public/Resources/Factsheets/Home_Modifications.aspx

In addition to the financing resources listed on that website, Medicaid can assist low-income homeowners with limited projects that will enable seniors to remain in their homes and keep them out of nursing homes. Medicaid is a federally-funded program administered by states to assist low-income persons with health care needs. States determine how they will allocate their funds, between home-based services and nursing home care. To be eligible, Medicaid recipients can have very few assets, which leads some people to 'spend down' their savings before applying for Medicaid. Consult a Medicaid advisor before you do this, though. The rules are complex. Find an advisor by calling your local Area Agency on Aging.

Another possible source of assistance for eligible veterans is the Veterans Administration. As with Eldercare and Medicare advisors, consult your local Area Agency on Aging. You can find it at https://www.n4a.org/

Finally, there is the option of using a home improvement loan or a reverse mortgage to finance a home improvement project.

Technology

There is an expectation that as Boomers age, they will bring their technology smarts into their older years. So far, this has not proven to be true. Older adults are not buying into the "Internet of Things," partly because of the expense of all these wired gadgets, and partly because of the learning curve associated with them. In general, older adults tend to resist change, but they do embrace technology they can afford and which they view as useful, such as email and Skype for keeping in touch with family.

There is one sector of the industry that is exploding, however, and that is technology related to aging.[13] This includes wearables and motion sensors and health-monitoring devices in the home, and transmission of data from such devices to caregivers and health care providers. Other devices can remind the resident when to take medication, to call for help when he/she needs assistance, to monitor visitors, or turn lighting on or off with motion sensors. These are just a few of the possibilities now available; each technology expo and trade show brings new ones.

There are two implications for aging in place with technology that need to be considered in a renovation project: one is that a strong WiFi signal is essential throughout the house. Some masonry and steel-framed multi-unit buildings may not have good reception in all areas. If you don't have good signal and cellphone reception, you need to determine how to get it. The second is an uninterrupted power supply. Do you have a home generator in case of power loss? This is essential where life-maintaining medical equipment is in use, and vital for maintaining health and comfort in emergency situations.

---

[13] The Aging in Place Technology website https://www.ageinplacetech.com/

Chapter 4: Relocating

Relocating away from your current community involves a lot more than picking a new place to live and then getting yourself there. It involves a move (gasp!) - serious sorting and packing, downsizing, getting rid of many years of accumulated stuff. It also requires adjusting to a new community, making new friends, and finding new stores, services, and doctors. Making new friends can be the biggest hurdle, and this gets more difficult as we age. In fact, adjusting to any change or disruption in our lives gets harder as we get older, and for frail, elderly people, a relocation can have serious physical and mental repercussions, no matter how beneficial the new facilities are.

But first let's talk about why you are considering putting yourself through this. The major reasons I hear in my workshops are:
- I want a different lifestyle such as beach, mountains, better weather, or even another country.
- I can't afford to retire in this expensive place - the taxes are too high.
- I want to be closer to my adult children and family.

So where to move? The old model had retirees moving to warm climates such as Florida or the Southwest. More recently, college towns, urban centers, and golf communities have gained favor. Some research cited by Stafford shows that relocation destinations often depend on existing ties to family or friends, or popular travel destinations. However, living somewhere is not the same as spending a few weeks in a place on vacation. One good piece of advice is to rent a place where you think you would like to live, and stay there for a year to see if it measures up to your expectations. One person, a liberal-minded academic from the Northeast, moved full-time to a southern city where he had vacationed for years. He found that the politics of the place were at odds with his views, and he never felt he fitted in with the community. Another person found that the heat and humidity of Florida summers were intolerable. A couple moved to a golf community, even though the husband (the golfer) was becoming increasingly limited in mobility, and the wife did not golf. A couple moved to a retirement community, and when the wife was widowed, she found that there were few activities for single women – the social events were all geared for couples.

Beyond the attributes of the destination, is the character of the specific neighborhood or even the site itself. These can vary widely even within the desired area. Clare Cooper Marcus cites the typology developed by Sidney Brower, Professor Emeritus in the School of Architecture, Planning, and Preservation at the University of Maryland in College Park. In it Brower proposes a three-part typology of residential settings: Big-Town, Small-Town and Out-of-Town. But this is not referring to the usual definitions of places as urban/suburban/rural. Rather, it refers to the way the place is experienced.

- Big-Town settings have places close to the home that are lively, stimulating, varied, open and tolerant.
- Small-town places offer nearby spaces that are familiar, stable, settled, where service is personal, and shops are locally run – the place where people know your name.

- Out-of-Town settings provide a buffer between the home and the neighbors, removed from the hustle and bustle of city life. The home is self-contained and preferred by people who want to be alone or only with selected friends and family members.

Thus, in deciding where you want to live, and where your spouse wants to live, consider how you both want to relate to the space outside your home, as well as what you want in the home itself.

So, what about that destination literature that I mentioned earlier? Most ratings are composites of weighted measurements on various dimensions. If you are making a decision based on ratings, you need to look at those dimensions and weights, and select the ones that are of interest to you. Averages and weighted composites don't represent your specific needs on a specific characteristic. What is it that gives your life meaning and purpose? That is what you need to be looking for. Will you find that in the place you are considering? A friend of mine was considering moving to a senior housing facility close to her son and his family. I asked her: "What is it that gives meaning to your life?" I didn't have to ask the second question because she said immediately: "I need to check out the church there."

Additionally, those ratings cover a large geographic area, sometimes a whole state, often a large city. There will be a large variation within that area on any dimension. State ratings are only valid on points common to the whole state, typically on taxes. You are not looking just for a city or area; you are looking for a community, a neighborhood, and a particular kind of housing. These can vary widely, even within an area that scores high on all your key factors. One factor not mentioned in the ratings is whether doctors in the area, both primary care and specialists, are accepting new Medicare patients. This can be a significant problem in areas with growing numbers of residents over 65.

Another question to ask is: Will this place be suitable for you when you reach the slow-go and the no-go years? If not, what will be your options at that time? Will you be able to make another move?

Some of the rating scales

The Milken Institute published a report titled *Best Cities for Successful Aging* in 2014. This report measures, compares, and ranks 352 U.S. metropolitan areas based on how well they enable older people to fulfill their potential, in their own lives as well as in their contributions to society and to others across the age spectrum. They included 84 indicators, grouped into 8 categories: general indicators such as cost of living, crime rate, weather, health care, wellness (recreational and healthy pursuits), financial, living arrangements, employment education, transportation and convenience, and community engagement. The full report is at
   http://successfulaging.milkeninstitute.org/2014/best-cities-for-successful-aging-report-2014.pdf

You can view the data and dig down into it at http://www.milkeninstitute.org/publications/view/671

WalletHub rated 150 largest cities for "retirement friendliness" in four categories: affordability, activities, quality of life, and health care.
https://wallethub.com/edu/best-places-to-retire/6165/.

This website also has access to ratings on other dimensions, such as pet-friendly cities.

If you envision staying in your new location through the slow-go and no-go years, check out AARP's Age-Friendly Communities. These are communities that are working to become great places for all ages, and to help older people stay in their own homes. AARP's network of livable communities is affiliated with the World Health Organization's Age-Friendly Cities and Communities Program. In AARP's words:

> AARP's participation in the program advances efforts to help people live easily and comfortably in their homes and communities as they age. AARP's presence encourages older adults to take a more active role in their communities and have their voices heard. Initiatives focus on areas such as housing, caregiving, community engagement, volunteering, social inclusion, and combating isolation among older citizens.[14]

AARP lists the eight domains of livability that contribute to an age-friendly community:

1. Outdoor spaces and buildings
2. Transportation
3. Housing
4. Social participation
5. Respect and social inclusion

---

[14] https://www.aarp.org/livable-communities/network-age-friendly-communities/info-2014/an-introduction.html

6. Civic participation and employment
7. Communication and information
8. Community and health services

A list of age-friendly communities can be found here: http://www.aarp.org/livable-communities/network-age-friendly-communities/info-2014/member-list.html

Living overseas

A small number of retirees opt to relocate out of the country. According to articles promoting the expatriate life, the primary motivation for overseas retirement is a lower cost of living, including low-cost quality health care. But there are other reasons, too. For some people, it is a love of a particular country or culture, a warmer climate, the desire for a different lifestyle, or a sense of adventure. Living abroad may be the retirement dream, but do your homework before you pack up and go.

This option is not for everyone. A Huffington Post article from editors of International Living listed seven questions to ask yourself to determine if you're cut out for overseas living:

Do you thrive on change?
Are you comfortable in new situations and with making new friends?
Are you okay with not living close to family?
Can you speak (or are you willing to learn) another language?
Are you intrigued by foreign cultures and customs?
Are you single, or if not, is your spouse or partner amenable to moving overseas?

Are you looking for a way to improve your quality of life while spending less money than you currently do?

Living overseas is not the same as being there on vacation. You will be dealing with the basic living issues while in a foreign environment. The social support network of friends and family, and the familiar products and services are not there. How will you manage your finances? Can you find medical care for your specific medical condition in the local area you are considering? Residency requirements can vary greatly from country to country, including laws regarding foreigners buying property. You may need to show proof of health insurance or the ability to support yourself. In most cases, Medicare will not cover your medical care out of the country.

Here is some advice from expats:

- Plan an extended stay in the area you are considering. A two-week vacation is not sufficient exposure to a place for such an important decision.
- Hire a tax professional specializing in international matters, especially the laws of the country you are planning to move to. Money crossing borders can create tax liabilities and other legal issues. You still must pay US taxes, and report foreign bank account balances over a certain amount to the IRS. In certain countries, you cannot receive Social Security payments.
- Hire an English-speaking lawyer locally for real estate purchases, wills and inheritance planning, and other legal matters. The US Embassy or Consulate can recommend some for you.

- Comfort is not the same as happiness. What is a *must* vs. what is *nice to have?* It won't be a lower cost retirement if you insist on doing it American style and buying imported American products.
- In spite of technology, Skyping with family and friends is not the same as being together. Your chosen location may be a place that the family would love to visit, but there is still the cost of their travel.

As was noted above, you are not just moving to a country, you will be living in a community, a neighborhood. Ratings are averages for the whole country or area, and should be read as such. *International Living* publishes an Annual Global Retirement Index. Ratings are based on the following points:

1. Cost and ease of renting or buying real estate.
2. Benefits and discounts available for pensioners
3. Visas and residence restrictions
4. Cost of living
5. Fitting in well with the local community
6. Entertainment and amenities such as the arts, sports, shopping
7. Quality and accessibility of health care
8. Healthy lifestyle
9. Infrastructure, including roads, water, air transit, internet, cellphone coverage, electrical service
10. Climate

Other publications include these in their ratings:

11. Time and ease of travel to US
12. Political stability, national and local laws, and third world bureaucracies

13. Lifestyle including languages, local customs – what is "normal" public behavior
14. Frequency of natural disasters

One way to live overseas is to volunteer. While many assignments are for a limited time, others can last for one or more years. It is a great way to get to know a culture and to help others. Below are several web sites to help you start your research on volunteering overseas (or voluntourism as it is sometimes called). Here are some websites to help you research overseas living and voluntourism.

- US State Department Bureau of Consular Affairs. Passport, visa and international travel information https://travel.state.gov/content/travel/en.html Also, Smart Traveler Enrollment Program. Register your trip with the nearest US embassy or consulate. https://step.state.gov/step/
- International Living: A blog with multiple writers providing information about relocating abroad. https://internationalliving.com/
- Live and invest overseas http://www.liveandinvestoverseas.com/
- https://bestplacesintheworldtoretire.com/
- Voluntourism.org http://www.voluntourism.org Integrates voluntary service in the nonprofit sector with the travel industry. Seeks to educate and engage travelers who want to engage in voluntourism, and offers numerous resources for travelers. Other options for skilled volunteers are http://www.teacherswithoutborders.org and http://www.worldteach.org. Also, the Peace Corps http://www.peacecorps.gov/

Second home

You may have purchased, or are thinking about purchasing a second home in a vacation spot, with the intention of living in it permanently after you retire. The same criteria in housing choice described above applies. These may conflict with your priorities for a vacation home. If you are thinking about purchasing a second home for eventual retirement as well as vacation use, you need to determine if the property is suitable for two, possibly conflicting uses. By the time you need to use the property for a permanent retirement home, a lot may change, including your health. A cabin in the mountains may be great for vacations but remoteness and inaccessibility won't work as you age. Do you know what the area is like year-round? Are all your neighbors snow-birds who won't be there most of the year? Are neighboring properties short-term rentals, sometimes to undesirable tenants? What is the community like off-season? Are there things to do or does the town shut down in the off-season? Will the resources and services you need be available and accessible during the off-season? How stable is your social support network there?

Chapter 5: Downsizing and Moving

Once you have made the decision to move to a smaller home, you face the task of downsizing and then making the move. You may look at a new, smaller place and think: "I can never fit in that small space!" In order to fit, you will need to get rid of all that accumulated stuff; however, your stuff is not you – having fewer possessions does not mean you are diminished as a person.

Yes. You can fit into a smaller space. Believe me! You learn to live a different lifestyle in a small space. The key is to put things away right away, and have an assigned place for everything. Keeping the clutter to a minimum is the big secret.

I moved to a senior living facility in 2014 and I got through it. Below are three blogs that I wrote originally for the Princeton Senior Resource Center and my own website, which relate my own journey through downsizing. There are some tips there for you, too.

Stuff (2011)

At the age of 92, Diana Athill, British editor and author, closed the flat where she had lived for many years and moved to a single room in a retirement home. Writing recently about her new downsized life, she said: . . .

> Nothing in the room is here out of habit, or because it was given me by dear old so-and-so, or because I couldn't be bothered to get rid of it. Everything, from the carpet to the biscuit tin and including of course the too many pictures, ornaments and books, is here because, however uninteresting it might be to others, I love it. It's as though 'pos-

sessing' has been distilled down from being a vague pleasure to being an intense one: less is more.

I was reminded of another quote: "Have nothing in your house that you do not know to be useful, or believe to be beautiful." That was from William Morris, an English architect, furniture, and textile designer associated with the English Arts and Crafts Movement.

I watched two friends struggle with downsizing for a move to smaller quarters, and saw how difficult it was to get rid of possessions that have accumulated over a long period of time. It made me look around my own house and see an accumulation of stuff that was neither beautiful nor useful. I have no intention of moving to smaller quarters, but still I got motivated to eliminate some of this stuff that I no longer have any use for. I vowed that when the time comes, I will have already found homes for it all, and won't have to resort to indiscriminate dumpsterizing.

Some things are easy to get rid of – old papers and magazines, books I will never read again, kitchen gadgets rarely used, clothes that no longer are appealing. (The clothes that no longer fit are a different story – they represent hope – of a leaner, more attractive self). This is a clue as to why this is so difficult: Some of our clutter represents our identity, our dreams, or image of self, our hopes for our future (hopefully thinner) selves.

Other things will take time to sort through and I will need to decide what to do with them. It looks like an overwhelming task, but I break it down and take it slowly, a drawer or a shelf at a time. I am making progress in the kitchen and a corner of the basement. The files of teaching materials are harder – I put a lot of myself into developing them, and my identity as a college professor is wrapped up there in those file drawers.

Having achieved a few empty drawers and shelves, I am resolved to keep them that way. This requires a change of thought process and resulting behavior. I see many lovely things in my volunteer time at Ten Thousand Villages, a shop selling handicrafts from third world countries. However, my new mind set is this: *Everything that comes into your house sooner or later will have to go out of your house, either by you or by somebody else. Do you really want this item?* Usually the answer is *no*.

I hope by the time I need to down size, I will be able, like Diana Athill, to have distilled my possessions down to only those I love. When I was a child, my mother made me iron my cotton batiste slips. I hated it, thought it a totally useless waste of time. I vowed I would never be ruled by my possessions. Less really is more. Less is freedom.

Stuff .. continued (2014)

Back in 2011, I wrote about Stuff - all those belongings that pile up and fill our homes. Now, as many of us are thinking about relocating and downsizing, all that accumulation of stuff can be a daunting obstacle. A few months ago, in the face of an impending blizzard, over 70 people came to hear our retirement speaker, Ellen Tozzi, talk about downsizing your possessions with ease.

That first article quoted Diana Athill who downsized from a flat to a one-room unit in a retirement home at the age of 92. She used the word 'distill' for the process – keeping only the things she truly loved and eliminating all the rest.

Well, now it is my turn, as I am moving from a large two-bedroom townhouse with a basement and garage to a small one-bedroom apartment. However, as I said in the first Stuff article, I have been working on downsizing for a few years, being motivated by watching other friends' struggles and hearing Ellen's talk numerous times. I can offer some advice from personal experience:

First, start long before you anticipate a move. When you go into a drawer or a shelf, look at what is there – all of it. See if there is anything there you have no further use for, and get rid of it right then and there. It only takes a few minutes, and little-by-little, the job will get done. For a serious downsizing project, Ellen advocates setting aside an hour or two at a specific time each week, rather than attempting to clean out the whole house at once. Most of my cupboards and closets had already been 'distilled' before I started the packing process. That made the job much easier, and far less stressful than it might have been.

Second, it can take multiple 'distillations' before you get to the essentials. What looked important in the first go-through may be less so when you have an actual picture of your future space. Often, I found myself thinking: *Why did I save this?*

Third, much of the material we have trouble parting with has to do with emotional connections with the past – papers, pictures, souvenirs of important occasions, connections with friends and family who may no longer be around. I had the most trouble with tossing teaching and consulting materials – there was very good stuff there! But their real meaning was in my professional identity as a college professor and hospitality consultant. I found that it was important to think about the future, rather than ruminating about the past. In my future place, I will not have room for all these files. But more important, I will never teach those courses again. I will be moving on to new and exciting opportunities, and I will use my new space for new activities. My self-image does not depend on those file drawers in the garage.

Stuff . . . continued 20 months later

So, here I am, 20 months post-move from an 1800 sq ft. two-bedroom townhouse with a basement and garage into a 900 sq ft one-bedroom condo with a 4x4' square storage locker. By the door is a large tub of fabric, bags of clothing and other miscellaneous items, plus two patio chairs ready to go a local church's spring rummage sale. And no, I did not over estimate how much stuff to move; I just got my get-rid muscles up to strength. I actually have extra room in the clothes closets and some drawers I am not using, but I have no reason to hang on to this stuff.

Once the habit is developed, getting rid of stuff that you no longer need comes naturally. In the case of the tub of fabric, I realized that I have no interest in sewing any more. I don't have the patience for large sewing projects, the agility and desire to crawl around on the floor to cut out patterns, or the eyesight for doing fine needlework. So, with that realization, getting rid of the fabric stash was a foregone conclusion. The dress patterns went out, too. I am keeping the sewing machine for mending projects, and some tubs of smaller pieces of fabric for a new project I want to take up: doll making.

The clothing is a different matter – this time, they are too big rather than too small and, since I have retired for the second time, I don't need a lot of dress-up outfits for presentations. If it isn't getting worn, it doesn't have to take up room in my closet.

Since the move, my life has become much simpler, and one reason is that there isn't all that stuff holding me back. The condo is small, but it holds everything I need. I just need to keep my get-rid muscles strong, because I know there will be new stuff coming in here from time to time, and I will need to keep things under control.

Resources for downsizing (or 'rightsizing') and moving

One could write a book on downsizing and moving, and a number of people have. I have listed several on the resource page at the end of the book. (You can get used copies at reduced prices from Amazon.com.)

There are people and businesses out there that have sprung up to help people make the transition to senior living. Professional organizers, like Ellen Tozzi mentioned above, will help you think through the process of sorting and getting rid of stuff. They know where to find new homes for things, and what needs to be trashed, and they can refer you to experts for valuing art and antiques. This is a growing field, and it has its own professional organization: National Association of Productivity & Organizing Professionals (NAPO). http://www.napo.net/. Hiring a decluttering professional is not cheap, but if you are overwhelmed by the task, it pays to bring in someone, even if for a few days to get you started. Once you get into the job, it will build momentum.

Senior Move Managers do more than help with downsizing. They specialize in helping older adults move to senior housing. In addition to the sorting and decluttering, they will plan and manage the entire move, including making the floor plan for the new home, arranging for movers, and doing all the packing and unpacking. They will also help with finding a realtor and preparing the house for sale. You can have them do the whole job, or contract for only parts of it, such as the packing and unpacking. You can find a Senior Move Manager through their association at National Association of Senior Move Managers at their website https://www.nasmm.org/find/index.cfm

This organization also has a helpful e-book called *It's So Much More than Moving: Your Guide to Stress-Free Right-Sizing and Relocation*. It covers all aspects of relocating and moving, including different types of senior housing. https://www.nasmm.org/education/guide_to_relocating.cfm

Chapter 6: Housing Options for the Go-Go years

Previous chapters have discussed aging in place - staying in your current home. There are other options for aging in place – another place that is more age-friendly. This new place can be in your current community or neighborhood, or elsewhere as previously discussed. Retirement communities for active, independent seniors go by different names, and sometimes are confused with assisted living. In fact, an on-line search for independent retirement housing will include listings for assisted living facilities. We will discuss the various types of care communities in Chapter 8. But here, let's discuss the options for the active go-go senior. Unless otherwise stated, these types of housing are not equipped to provide any kind of care services.

55 plus or age-restricted communities

Under the Housing for Older Persons Act of 1995, a community may market itself as restricted to persons age 55 or older and not be in violation of the Federal Fair Housing Act. At least one resident of a unit must be over the age of 55. Communities may set higher limits as well. Individuals below the age of 19 cannot live in the unit, and there may be regulations as to how long young children can stay on a visit.

- **Active Adult Communities.** These often resemble resorts, with a wide range of amenities and activities offered in a clubhouse, which may include a swimming pool, exercise rooms, golf, tennis, art, educational and cultural programs, clubs, and trips. Each living unit has a full kitchen, but dining services may be offered, often with menus and service comparable with fine restaurants. Usually there are various meal plans offered, and residents can choose when and where they dine. Housekeeping, landscaping, and maintenance are provided, freeing the resident to enjoy the facilities. Residences may be apartments in a multi-unit building, freestanding cottages, villas or townhouses, or a combination of all types. Some independent living communities are a part of a Continuing Care Retirement Community (CCRC) which is described in a later section. Others are stand-alone developments. Social services are usually not provided in active adult communities, but there may be an activities or program director.

- **Senior Living Communities.** These terms are loosely used, but typically, senior living facilities provide fewer amenities than the active adult communities. In either case, a program of activities is provided, as is exterior maintenance of the facility. A senior living facility may be rental units; some offer condominiums which residents can purchase. Some may offer affordable housing units for those who qualify. Senior living facilities are run either by a non-profit organization or a for-profit corporation; condominium communities are run by the residents through their homeowner association.
- **Cooperatives.** In a co-op, a corporation owns the property, and residents own shares of the corporation. They pay a monthly fee which covers the mortgage, insurance, taxes, and operating costs. The resident

association usually hires a management company to manage the facility. Thus, in a condo association, residents own real estate, which is marketed, taxed, and financed as regular housing. Co-op residents do not own real estate, they own shares of a corporation which pays mortgage interest and real estate taxes. The corporation must then inform the share owners of the mortgage interest and taxes attributable to their unit.

- **Congregate Housing.** While not designed for the go-go years, congregate housing offers independent units with common social areas and some services provided such as one meal a day. Funded by the U.S. Department of Housing and Urban Development, the congregate facility's purpose is to enable older, frail, low-income adults to remain independent as long as possible and reduce or prevent nursing home stays. Some social services may be offered on the premises.

Alternatives to independent senior housing

With the market for senior housing growing as the population ages, individuals and developers are coming up with more and more alternatives to suit people with different needs, interests, and income levels. Some are quite quirky, others make a lot of sense.

- Cohousing is a small but growing movement. The Cohousing Association of the United States http://www.cohousing.org/ defines cohousing as an intentional community of private homes clustered around a shared space. The key words are *intentional* and *community*. That shared space includes a common kitchen and dining area, laundry facilities and spaces for recreational programs as well as common outdoor spaces. Members of the community have independent incomes and lives, but share some meals, recreational activities and upkeep duties. These communities are small, typically 20-40 homes. They are organized as a home-owner association, managed by the residents. Cohousing communities have not been age-restricted in the past, but there are now about 25 senior cohousing communities completed or under construction.

- Home sharing was mentioned above as a way to reduce housing cost. There are other advantages to sharing a house with other compatible people, primarily the companionship offered, and the availability of others, if and when you need help. This cannot be overestimated. The key word here is compatibility. There are programs that screen and match home-sharers. The National Shared Housing Resource Center (NSHRC) lists such programs at http://nationalsharedhousing.org/program-directory/ They also have resources for home-sharers.
- Niche developments designed for a specific group of people. A residence for retired actors and singers was portrayed in the movie *Quartet*; such facilities really do exist. The Motion Picture & Television industry has had such a facility since 1942, and there are others. Unions and fraternal organizations have had homes for their elder members for many years as have religious denominations. These have typically been for lower income members, or members without family support. More

recently, real estate developers have been entering this market with a wide variety of upscale facilities designed for nationality groups such as Indians or Chinese, or members of the gay and lesbian community. Other communities are not limited, but designed to appeal to a specific particular group such golfers or university alumni. Jimmy Buffett is developing Margaritaville senior living communities for people who grew up on his music. Stay tuned: who knows what's next!

- Mobile homes or manufactured housing in age-restricted parks. This option has also been around for many years, particularly in Florida and the Sun Belt. These parks provide low-cost housing and community, typically in an attractive resort area. Usually, residents own their houses but pay rent for the use of the land, which is privately owned.
- The tiny house movement is, well, tiny but growing. Millennials and Boomers are the primary markets, both facing the increasing costs of housing while trying to live on a limited income. However, the tiny house movement is about more than cost, it is about a simplified lifestyle and preserving the environment. Tiny houses are typically 100 to 500 square feet; they are often on wheels so they can be relocated. This gets around zoning restrictions in many communities – they are not fixed to the land. Tiny houses are suitable for able-bodied people, but they are not so well suited for elders with mobility limitations, since typically the sleeping area is in a loft accessible by ladder. Here is a website on tiny houses:

http://www.investopedia.com/articles/investing/092815/tiny-house-movement-making-market-opportunities.asp

- R-Vs. There is a small but avid community of folks who have given up permanent housing to live in their RV or motor home and travel the country. They often have friends on the road with them, and they meet up in various locations. Some travel in order to take seasonal jobs in parks or resorts. Others may work remotely from where ever they happen to be. Some do it because they love the travel, others because they cannot afford permanent housing.
- Extended-stay hotels can become de-facto senior housing. Budget hotels do offer long term discounted rates to seniors, especially if the hotel is experiencing low occupancy rates. There is concern in some communities that such housing may be in decline and may not offer the residents the safety, services, and socialization they need.
- Cruise ships. A few sea-worthy seniors have found homes at sea on cruise ships. They claim that the discounted rates for long sails are not that much more than a luxury senior housing facility, and they get to travel the world. The cruise ship offers all the amenities they would get in a luxury senior facility; in addition, they develop close relationships with the crew members.

I don't wanna live with a bunch of old people

This may be the strongest argument one can have for aging in place in his or her own home. Let's look at what is behind it. Some people express a strong preference for living in a community with people of diverse ages. They enjoy being around young people and children. This works well for all concerned, as long as the community continues to provide social support, interactions, and services as the older person ages. The children are exposed to older folks and young people benefit from gaining the perspective of their elders.

But, behind this statement may be the stereotyped view that all people living in senior housing are frail, sick, demented, and dying. And, yes, people in senior housing do age and die, as do we all. Also, the older housing developments tend to have an older population than the more recently built ones. But you will also find a wide range of abilities and disabilities in senior living, including folks who have had fascinating life experiences and are still vital and active.

Another factor may be the fear of labeling oneself as "old" – a matter of personal identity. Who am I? Well, I am not an "old person." At some point, we need to face reality. When will you do that? When you have a major health crisis? At that point, it is too late to make plans for the next step, and you are forced to deal with the reality and the limitations imposed by the crisis.

Two views of senior living:
> One woman said: "I like living with my peers. We are all dealing with the same issues of aging. We understand each other, and we help each other."
>
> Another said: "I open my door and see the walkers and wheelchairs going past. That is my future, and it isn't pretty."

Both of these women live in the same community.

How do people in senior housing communities deal with this phenomenon? I have come up with several strategies:

- Keep involved with the wider community, and don't get totally immersed in the senior living facility. There is a wider world out there and we need to keep it in perspective.
- There are active, vital, and interesting people of varying ages living in senior communities. Identify them and make them your models. I don't like the phrase 'young at heart' but that is what these people are, and we can learn a lot about living from them.
- View the frailer residents as reminders and motivators for healthy living – exercising, eating well, controlling weight, staying positive in our attitudes. While we all age, there is a lot we can do to "*live young while growing old, and to die young, as late as possible.*" That is, to increase the 'health span' by adopting a healthy lifestyle, thus delaying the onset of frailty and dependency.

Continuing care retirement communities (CCRCs)

CCRCs offer various levels of housing and services, including independent living in individual villas, cottages, or apartments, assisted living, nursing home facilities and memory care (Alzheimer's and dementia) units, all on the same campus. These various components are described in greater detail below. What the CCRC is really offering is security and peace of mind. There is a recent move in the industry to change its name to Life Plan Community, thinking that this is more appealing to younger retirees. This doesn't seem to have caught on yet, but you may find some communities that use this term.

In most CCRCs, you do not own your unit; you receive a package of services including the right to occupy a specific unit, plus some or all meals, housekeeping, utilities, maintenance, and activities. You still maintain your independence in your own unit and can come and go as you please. Depending on the type of contract you choose, you may pay a (usually sizeable) entry fee, plus a monthly service fee which covers the cost those services listed above. The monthly maintenance fee will be based on the location and size of the residential unit and the services provided. To be accepted as a resident, you may have to demonstrate that you have sufficient financial resources to afford to live there, and you will have to be physically fit – medically approved - when you move in. Thus, it may not pay to wait until you have a health crisis to make the move. By then, you may not qualify. I will discuss CCRC terms and contracts below.

About 80 percent of CCRC's are run by non-profit organizations, many of them faith-based, but for-profit corporations are moving into this field. In either case, residents do not have much of a say in how the place is managed.

The advantages of a CCRC
- While you may move from your independent living unit to a care unit as your needs dictate, you do not have to leave the community and the friends you have made there. This is particularly helpful when

one spouse needs a higher level of care, such as the nursing care unit, while the other spouse can remain in the home unit, close by and still able to maintain independence, while visiting the nursing care unit at any time. For others, the nursing unit is available on a temporary basis for rehab following a hospitalization, after which the resident returns to the independent housing unit.

- A big appeal of a CCRC is the number of services provided, typically in a luxurious setting. Residents don't have to worry about house cleaning, snow shoveling, lawn mowing, or home maintenance, and that is a big selling point. Also, there are usually many amenities – swimming pool, spa, tennis courts, putting greens, gym, walking paths, card rooms, games, libraries, programs and activities, classes and cultural events, trips, local transportation, and restaurant-quality meals with a choice of meal plans and types of service. Personal services such as a bank, barber and hair salon, and limited shopping are usually available on-site. Some doctors and other health care specialists may maintain offices and see patients on the campus.
- Most CCRC's, especially those run by nonprofits, will not evict residents if they outlive their money through no fault of their own. This may not be advertised, but it is an appealing feature for people who have that concern. (This feature may be referred to as a Life Plan Community).

The downsides of a CCRC
- The CCRC industry and senior housing suffered from the housing market collapse in 2009. Prospective residents could not sell their homes, so they could not move into the new senior housing developments that had been constructed earlier in the decade. Thus, for a few years, the industry was financially unstable, and some large operators went bankrupt. This is worrisome for this type of arrangement, since the residents usually do not own equity in their units, but rather pay a significant entry fee as a deposit.
- Another issue facing the industry is the rising cost of health care. Delivery of health care services in their assisted living and nursing home units has an impact on the CCRC's bottom line, which produces increasing service fees beyond increases for general inflation.
- A third issue is the question of whether CCRCs operated by nonprofit organizations are exempt from property taxes. This issue is being challenged in many counties, and the outcomes could impact service fees in the future.
- Life in a CCRC can become very self-contained. Because almost everything you could want is offered on-site, it is easy to exist 'in a bubble'; you rarely need to leave the campus. Many CCRCs were built outside of metropolitan areas where land was cheap, and therefore it may be a trip to get to shopping malls, doctors' offices, theaters, public libraries, and other city attractions. If you don't drive,

the CCRC will usually provide transportation to local doctors' offices and some scheduled transportation to select destinations, but you will have to go on their schedule or pay an extra charge.
- Because of the lower land cost, many CCRCs are low-rise buildings – one or two stories, but spread out over substantial acreage. For people with mobility issues, access to the dining rooms and activity areas could be very difficult. Some may resort to wheel chairs or scooters before they really need them, and this contributes to a downward spiral of lost mobility.
- The big attraction of a CCRC is the availability of a continuum of care. However, the timing and transition from one to another may be difficult, and the resident (or the family) may not have a say in the matter. Some residents may want to stay in their independent living unit with a home health care aide. You, the prospective resident, need to ask what is the policy on this issue, and under what conditions the CCRC will require you to move. Also, what is the guarantee that a bed will be available in the unit you need to move to? When you need to move to a care unit, your options are those operated by your CCRC. They may or may not offer the quality of services you want. You can go elsewhere, but you would not receive the cost benefit from your CCRC (which you have been contributing to).
- CCRCs are age-restricted communities. Persons younger that the stated age may visit for a short time, but are not permitted to live there. This pre-

cludes the possibility of grandparents raising grandchildren in a CCRC.
- When new CCRC developments (or other age-restricted communities) are first built, they tend to attract younger residents. As the facility fills up, those residents age in place. When the units start to turn over, the population is older, and the place is less attractive to younger people. Thus, you need to be comfortable with the general age of the population in the development you are considering.

AARP has an extensive checklist of questions to ask when you are evaluating a CCRC:

http://www.aarp.org/relationships/caregiving-resource-center/info-09-2010/ho_what_to_ask_retirement_communities.2.html

AARP also has a directory of all types of senior housing at http://search.seniorliving.aarp.org/

CCRC contracts

One expert in the industry has called the CCRC contract "the most complicated legal document a consumer will ever sign." If you are considering a move to a CCRC, it is essential that you have a lawyer, who is knowledgeable in senior housing and CCRCs, to review your contract and explain it to you before you sign it. Do not rely on the sales representative's word.

There are various types of contracts, and what a community is offering depends on how the management views the local market demand, competition, and current economy. The entrance fee and monthly service charge will vary for individual units within the community, depending on the size and location of the unit. There is a second, lesser monthly charge for a second person in the unit. In general, there are three types of contracts:

Type A: Extensive or Life Care Contract. Residents pay an entrance fee, which may be substantial, plus a monthly service charge. This charge will rise over time to cover inflationary costs. All housing, services, and amenities are provided. If the resident moves to a care facility, he or she will pay a set monthly service charge, which is discounted from the market rate; it may be more or less than the service charge they were paying for their independent living unit. A portion of the upfront entrance fee is applied to cover the difference between the discounted rate and the market rate. If the entrance fee is ultimately used up to cover this cost difference, the resident may continue to stay there without additional charges. Communities that offer this may call themselves a "Life Care Community," and be subject to a higher level of financial regulation by the state. The appeal of this type of contract is predictability regarding the cost of care facilities.

A portion of the monthly charge may qualify as an IRS medical deduction, as it is a prepayment of medical costs. Also, a portion of the entrance fee may be deductible in the year it is paid.

Type B: Modified or Continuing Care Contract. This is similar to Type A except that use of the care facilities is limited to a specified number of days and/or level of discounted cost, after which the resident is responsible for the cost of the additional care. The entrance fee is lower than in the Type A contract. As with the Type A contract, a portion of the monthly charge and entrance fee may qualify as an IRS medical deduction.

Type C: Fee-For-Service Contract. Access to the health care facilities is guaranteed, but the resident must pay the full market rate for the services they use. This option is more popular with residents who have long-term care insurance. Some communities do charge an entrance fee for a Type C contract and apply it to care costs until it runs out. Residents with a Type C contract do not qualify for an IRS medical deduction.

Rental: Residents pay month-to-month rent, and full market rates if they move to any of the care facilities.

Direct Admissions. Some communities admit individuals directly to their care facilities. They pay full cost for the level of service.

Because you may have a sizeable entrance fee on deposit with the community, you need to be sure that it is financially stable. Entrance fees should be kept in escrow accounts and not applied to current operating costs, except to subsidize residents' stays in the care facility, as per their contract. Ask for financial statements and have your lawyer review them. State oversight of CCRCs can vary considerably. Find out what the required reserve levels are in the state you are considering, and if the community meets them. What provision is made to safeguard residents' entrance fee deposits in the case of bankruptcy or sale of the property?

The Commission on Accreditation of Rehabilitation Facilities (CARF) has an extensive publication of CCRC financing: *Consumer Guide to Understanding Financial Performance and Reporting in Continuing Care Retirement Communities.* You can download it at:
http://www.carf.org/Resources/ConsumerResources/

Refundable entrance fees

All three contract types may come with a refundable option for the entrance fee, and the size of that fee will be impacted by the refundable option you select – the higher the refundable, the higher the initial fee. This is an important consideration. Not everyone leaves a CCRC by death. They move out for other reasons, a prime one is to be nearer to adult children and family. However, either way you leave, dead or alive, you or your estate may get a refund depending on your contract. There may be a time limit, after which there is no refund, and there may be a lag between the time you leave and when you receive your refund.

Types of refunds:
- 100% refund. Most popular in newly built communities that need to build up-front capital, through higher entrance fees. Typically, a community cannot get funding to start building until a certain number of units have been sold.
- 50% refund or some other level in between.
- Declining balance. The amount of the refund is reduced by a certain percentage, up to a specified period of time, after which there is no refund.
- Market value. This is based on the determined value of the unit at the time the resident vacates.
- Nonrefundable. This is the most economical option, with no addition to the entrance fee.

Chapter 7: Slow-Go and No-Go Years

At some point, a fast pace of travel, work, volunteering, and activity starts to take a toll on an aging body, and we find ourselves slowing down a bit. The slow-go years are an adjustment to aging. We may still travel, but less frequently and on shorter trips. We opt for a little less rigor in our exercise, and cut back on work or volunteer hours. We start looking for outside help with chores such as lawn care and snow removal. And, eventually, at least some of us will need some level of care. Where do we find the help we need? If you are aging in place – in your home – probably the first kind of help you would look for is home maintenance – housecleaning and yard work, or possibly transportation assistance. Here are some resources:

- **Naturally Occurring Retirement Communities (NORCs).** The Congressional Research Service defines a NORC as a "community with a sizeable proportion of older persons (typically 55 to 65 and up) residing within a specified geographic area." This could mean anything from a zip code to an apartment building. The requirements for a NORC can vary from state to state, but typically, NORCs are areas in which at least 40 percent of heads of households are over 60 years of age. Where this occurs, the community, the residents, or non-profit agencies may organize to provide social services and support to that population through a NORC-SSP, a non-profit organization (or a network of non-profits), funded with government, private donations, and/or member dues. NORC-SSPs provide services such as educational, recreation, health care management, case management, or transportation to the residents of the area at a location convenient to them or in their own homes. They may provide members with access to discounted or volunteer-provided services such as home maintenance, transportation or cleaning services.

- **Villages.** Villages are non-profit member organizations that have sprung up to help older members access services they need to remain in their own homes. While there is no uniform model of how a village operates, usually, there is a mix of paid staff and volunteers, and funding is through member dues. The members served are encouraged to volunteer also, to the extent they are able. Besides assisting members with services, villages also provide social activities to minimize isolation, build community, and promote wellness. You can find out if there is a village program in the area you are considering at Village to Village Network http://vtvnetwork.org
- **Area Agencies on Aging.** Local Area Agencies on Aging were established by the Older Americans Act of 1973. Their mission is to develop, coordinate, and deliver services to older Americans and their caregivers in every local community. Your local Agency on Aging office can provide valuable information about what services are available in your area and how to access them. Find it at https://www.n4a.org/
- **The Eldercare Locator**, a service of the Administration on Aging, also has a website where you can find organizations and services for older adults in

your community.
http://www.eldercare.gov/Eldercare.NET/Public/Index.aspx

Home services and home health care

At some point, the older adult may need more than housekeeping and lawn mowing services – he or she may need some level of personal care. Home care was mentioned earlier as part of the age-in-place option. The first line of defense is unpaid care delivered by a spouse, adult child, or other relative. Even this is not cost-free, however. The caregiver may have given up work income to provide the care. Some states are now providing small Family Caregiving grants to low-income family caregivers who are able to keep their elders at home and out of a nursing home. But still, there are the hidden and not so hidden costs of medications, medical equipment and consumable items, transportation to doctors and therapists, and occasional respite care. There is another hidden cost – the stress and drain on the strength of the caregiver, who may be caring for her own children, or else the care giver is a spouse or sibling who is up in years, too. A response to this is to hire a caregiver, either part-time or full-time.

An individual may hire a care assistant, but more likely, it is a spouse or family member who seeks to hire an aide. The other avenue is a hospital ordering home care as part of a patient's discharge-to-home requirement. Hospitals are under pressure from Medicare and are penalized if a recently discharged patient is readmitted for the same condition they had previously. Therefore, hospitals work to ensure that the discharged patient is going to an environment where the patient will receive the type of care needed, and they will provide recommendations for home care agencies.

Types of care in the home

- Companion. Provides "fellowship and protection" as per the Department of Labor definition. That includes socializing, engaging in social and mental activity, accompanying to social events and exercise, and being available so that the client is not left alone. Companions do not provide any personal care or housekeeping services.
- Homemaker. Performs housekeeping duties such as cooking, light housekeeping, laundry, pet care, errands, and driving to appointments and activities. Homemakers do not perform personal care tasks for the senior. Some long-term care insurance policies may pay some of the cost of a homemaker. Veterans' benefits may also be available to those who qualify.
- Home Care. Custodial care, which includes assistance with such tasks as bathing, dressing, medication reminders, laundry, meal preparation, pet care, running errands, or driving to doctor appointments or social events. The home care aide does not provide any medical care. The position may be called personal care or attendant care. Medicare does not pay for custodial care. Medicaid may pay for certain aspects of home care if it allows a low-income senior to remain in his or her own home. Some long-term care insurance policies and veterans' benefits may pay some of these costs.

- Home Health Care. Requires medical training. May include such tasks a checking vital signs, assistance with braces, ventilation equipment, artificial limbs, injections, wound care, medication management, and monitoring serious illness or unstable conditions. Medicare will cover those services if the person is confined to the home, and the services are provided under a doctor's order.
- Visiting Nurses. Nurse practitioners and physicians' assistants and other professionals, such as physical therapists, or social workers. This is covered by Medicare if under a doctor's order.

The home health care industry is the fastest growing sector of the US labor market. The Bureau of Labor Statistics estimated that the field would grow from 1.2 million jobs in 2014 to over 2 million in 2024. At the same time, an AARP Public Policy Institute Report showed that the caregiver ratio – the ratio of potential caregivers ages 45-64 to persons over 80 is declining and will continue to do so. In 1990, the ratio was 6.6 and the report projected that by 2030 it would be down to 4.1, and by 2050 to 2.9. This is bad news in the face of the growing population of older adults. At the same time, the labor market for caregivers is increasingly composed of foreign-born workers, which is threatened by the current presidential administration's policies on immigration. Home care positions are among the lowest paying jobs, and are often demanding and stressful, hardly attractive to many jobseekers. There is a large turnover in this type of work.

So, where are you going to find a caregiver? AARP reports that 2/3 of Americans believe they can rely on family members to meet their long-term support needs. However, family sizes are shrinking, and adult children are often living at considerable distances from aging parents. There are costs of family caregiving as noted above. Another consideration is the increasing level of medical needs of the older population. Family members simply may not be able to provide the complex care that their elders require.

Some seniors do not require a single service, but rather a whole range of services, including lawn care, home maintenance, pet walkers, visiting nurses, Meals on Wheels, grocery delivery, car services, and concierge or errand runners. Hiring an aide to provide all these services is not the end of the problem. Aides quit, go on vacation, can't work the necessary schedule, don't fit with in the family, or are not compatible with the care recipient. These services all need to be coordinated. The person to do this is a geriatric care manager (sometimes called a case manager).

Geriatric care managers

The Aging Life Care Association (formerly the National Association of Professional Geriatric Care Managers) defines a geriatric care manager as "a health and human services specialist who acts as a guide and advocate for families who are caring for older relatives or disabled adults." Families or elderly clients hire geriatric care managers to oversee every aspect of care. Geriatric care managers assess clients' needs, make a care plan, coordinate care, and oversee the care that is given. The medical needs of the client are only a small aspect of the care that geriatric care managers oversee. Geriatric care managers are especially helpful when family members live at a distance from their elderly relatives and cannot easily check in or oversee the care. Geriatric care managers earn certifications through Aging Life Care. You can learn more about this valuable service and find a geriatric care manager in your area at https://www.aginglifecare.org. As a part of their service, they will assist you in finding the right services and aides.

Hiring a home care or home health care aide

Some families choose to hire their own aide, thinking they can avoid paying agency rates, or else they already know someone who has been recommended to them. Unless you are prepared to do significant background and criminal history checking, this can be risky. There are far too many cases of individuals gaining access to seniors' homes in the guise of caregiving, only to steal their money and abuse them. Nevertheless, there are cases where private hires have worked out beautifully, and even formed a strong bond with their client and family. Don't forget, though, that while you may consider the person a member of the family, you are not part of the aide's family. The aide may have family obligations that he or she must attend to before attending to your needs. If the aide cannot work due to illness or family needs, you must find the substitute or provide the care yourself. You are also vulnerable to aides walking off the job as a demand for higher wages, or, if they are foreign born, immigration problems.

If you hire someone directly, you are responsible for paying them and for managing federal and state, and possibly local payroll taxes, including withholding and FICA (Social Security), plus liability insurance and workers compensation insurance. This means withholding from the employee's pay. You may also have to pay federal and state unemployment taxes. You must file and remit quarterly federal withholding and social security taxes (employee and employer), sometimes called the "Nanny Tax." Note that FICA is levied on both the employer and the employee. This is a complicated process, and there is software on the market to help you with the calculations and the reporting. You may find someone in your community who runs a business doing this kind of reporting for household employers. It is worth the cost to have this done for you. Some agencies require that in addition to the check you write to pay your employee, you send a check to the agency for the taxes, and they will handle the filing and paperwork. For information on the federal taxes, consult IRS Publication 926. For state taxes, consult your state Department of Taxation.

Home care and home health aides are considered domestic service workers by the Federal Wage and Hour Division of the Department of Labor, under the Fair Labor Standards Act. They must be paid at least the federal minimum wage, currently $7.25/hour and time and a half for hours over 40 in a work week. State and local laws may require a higher minimum rate, and the going market rate in your area is probably higher. Foreign-born aides must have proper credentials to work in the United States.

Live-in aides must be paid at least the minimum wage, and are subject to the overtime rates over 40 hours in a work week. You must keep track of hours worked, and allow for meal times, breaks, and sleep time. However, if their duties are limited to companionship and "protection" (just being present in case of emergency), they may be exempt from overtime rates. However, they still must

be paid for all hours worked. The law is complex. If you have hired a live-in aide, consult Federal Wage and Hour Fact Sheets 79 A-E. Below are links to Fact Sheet 79 B Live-in Domestic Service Workers, and Fact Sheet 79A on Companion Services.
https://www.dol.gov/whd/regs/compliance/whdfs79b.htm
https://www.dol.gov/whd/regs/compliance/whdfs79a.htm

Hiring through an agency

Hiring through an agency has its advantages, although agency rates are higher. However, there are different types of agencies providing different levels of service. If you are hiring a health aide to perform duties that Medicare will cover, you need to use a Medicare-certified agency. Find the ones in your area at https://www.medicare.gov/ home-healthcompare/search.html

Similarly, if the services are covered by Medicaid, you need a Medicaid-certified agency.

Licensed health care services firms' personnel are employees of the agency, screened, trained and paid by the agency, which handles all the tax withholding and filing functions. These employees will be licensed and supervised by a registered nurse or similarly qualified person. If the aide is unable to work a shift, the agency will send a substitute. This contrasts with an agency which is only an employment or job registry. Employees coming through such a registry are independent contractors, and you must pay them as described above for private hires. The agency may handle the tax filing duties, and require you to send them a check for the withheld and FICA taxes.

The Family Caregiver Alliance has a useful guide for hiring home care and home health care aides. Their website at www.caregiver.org has a number of useful resources for caregivers.

https://www.caregiver.org/hiring-home-help

Medicare also has a check list for choosing a home health care agency at https://www.medicare.gov/what-medicare-covers/home-health-care/Home%20Health%20Agency%20Checklist.pdf

Chapter 8: Care Facilities - Assisted Living and Nursing Homes

Before we talk about care facilities, we should define the activities of daily living (ADLs). It is how the older person scores on these various activities that determines what level of care he or she requires. These activities do not require skilled nursing care, and therefore the costs of providing care are not covered by Medicare. There are two different screenings, which are typically performed by professionals in the field: *ADLs* and *Instrumental Activities of Daily Living (IADLs)*.

ADLs involve self-care and include the ability to:
- Dress oneself
- Use the toilet (not incontinent)
- Feed oneself
- Bathe/maintain personal hygiene
- Ambulate – walk independently or transfer into or out of a car, wheelchair, and bed

IADLs are those that enable individuals to function independently in the community:
- Meal preparation
- Housework
- Shopping
- Use transportation (car, public or arranged rides)
- Manage medications
- Handle money

There are several screening instruments that professionals use to evaluate an older person's needs. A reduction of ability on one or two points may not indicate a need to move to a care facility if alternative support is available. For instance, Meals on Wheels may be a substitute for the inability to prepare meals.

Facilities such as assisted living residences and nursing homes use ADL screenings to determine if a potential resident would benefit from their services, what care level would be required, hence what the fee would be. Medicaid, which is federally funded but state-based, uses ADL screenings to determine eligibility. Medicaid has income level criteria. Medicare does not pay for care to maintain ADL levels. Here are some examples of screening instruments for ADLs and IADLs

http://www.unmc.edu/media/intmed/geriatrics/reynolds/pearlcards/functionaldisability/IADLs_form.pdf

http://clas.uiowa.edu/socialwork/files/socialwork/NursingHomeResource/documents/Katz%20ADL_LawtonIADL.pdf

https://www.payingforseniorcare.com/longtermcare/activities-of-daily-living.html

One caveat here: my social worker contacts tell me that if you visit these various care facilities, you may see residents who don't appear to fit the admission criteria. These residents probably did fit when they were admitted; however, their conditions have changed, but they have not been moved. At an advanced age, any move or change could bring on relocation trauma and have severe consequences.

How likely is it that I will need care?

The US Department of Health and Human Services has published the following statistics on the types of care, duration, and percent of people who use each type of care.

Remember, these are averages; someone turning 65 today has almost a 70% chance of needing some type of long-term care services and support in their remaining years. Women need care longer (3.7 years) than men (2.2 years). One-third of today's 65-year-olds may never need long-term care support, but 20 percent will need it for longer than 5 years.

Distribution and duration of long-term care services
U.S. Department of Health and Human Services
www.LongTermCare.gov   10/10/2017

Type of care	Average number of years people use this type of care	Percent of people who use this type of care (%)
Any Services	3 years	69
At Home		
Unpaid care	1 year	59
Paid care	Less than 1 year	42
Any care at home	2 years	65
In Facilities		
Nursing facilities	1 year	35
Assisted living	Less than 1 year	13
Any care in facilities	1 year	37

Controlling the decision

Stephen Golant has written that older people who have had input into decisions about their lives and environments are more satisfied with their new arrangements, have better physical and mental health, and enjoy an overall higher quality of life. This includes having input into the choice, having time to prepare, and visiting their new quarters. When others have made the housing decision for them, the outcome is far less satisfactory, especially if the move has been made quickly. The result can be a decline in physical health, increased anxiety, depression and loneliness, and a strong sense of loss and related grief. They may feel rushed, coerced, punished, or dumped.

While the older person may not be capable of making the decision, he or she can choose to delegate it to another, trusted person. They are still in control as they have named someone to make that decision; this leads to greater satisfaction with the outcome.

The following sections describe the various types of care facilities that older adults may need. Terminology may vary in various areas of the country, and licensing requirements and standards can differ from state to state. Check with the Area Agency on Aging for the area you are considering.

Assisted living

There is no standard definition of term 'assisted living,' but in general, it is a form of care facility for people who need a bit of help with some of the ADLs or IADLs (often medication management), but not continuous medical or custodial care. Regulation of assisted living facilities is done at the state level, and can vary widely. In some states, facilities offering assisted living may not be licensed or regulated, and they may or may not offer some services. Facilities can vary widely from a small board and care home with just a few beds to an elegant facility that looks more like a resort hotel. These types of facilities offer a variety of floor plans, including some apartment-sized units. However, since three meals a day are provided, these units usually only have limited kitchen facilities; perhaps only a small refrigerator and a microwave. Residents can bring their own furnishings. All housekeeping services are provided, along with a social activities program. Laundry services are available for a separate charge. A nurse is available to manage medications.

There is a base charge for room and board, plus additional charges based on the level of care the resident needs. Medicare does not cover the cost of assisted living; Medicaid coverage is available in some states, and the Veterans Administration will pay for eligible veterans.

Assisted living facilities follow a social model rather than a medical model. They provide a secure environment with nonmedical services, including personal care, preventive health services, and planned social and recreational activities. There may be a memory care unit with specially trained staff.

Assisted living facilities may also offer short-term respite care for people who are cared for in their homes. Respite care gives caregivers a break from their duties, and it also allows the older person a chance to experience the facility if the family is considering moving him or her there. Respite units are fully furnished.

AARP has a checklist to evaluate these facilities at http://assets.aarp.org/www.aarp.org_/promotions/text/life/AssistedLivingChecklist.pdf

Residential care homes and adult foster care homes

Board and care homes, sometimes called group homes, provide the same services as assisted living facilities; the difference being that they are smaller, typically in a private home setting. The home may have only a few residents, as few as four to six, although some may have as many as twenty. They may also have a wider age range of residents, but all require some level of assistance. In most states, residential care homes must be licensed.

The advantages of residential care homes are:
- Smaller, more intimate setting
- More individualized attention from staff
- May be significantly less expensive than an assisted living facility
- A less structured, institutional setting

The disadvantages include:
- Fewer amenities and services offered
- Fewer residents to socialize with
- Residents have their own bedroom which may be shared rather than a full apartment

Nursing homes

Chances are that if you need a nursing home, you will not be making the choice – your family member, health proxy, or power of attorney will be making that decision. It helps, however, to know what the alternatives are, the costs, and the available facilities.

Nursing homes offer two types of services:
- Skilled nursing care and short-term rehabilitation services such as physical or occupational therapy, sometimes called sub-acute care or rehabilitation. This may include care during recovery from surgery, illness, injury, or a terminal illness, after which the patient is discharged to home or possibly to another type of care facility. Such patients do not need hospital care, but they do need 24-hour care and monitoring of their condition. Skilled nursing care includes a medical plan based on diagnoses, and monitoring by a team of health care professionals. Skilled nursing facilities may also offer short-term respite care or custodial respite care.
- Custodial care for people who need assistance with some or all of the ADLs, on a 24-hour basis. They do not need skilled nursing care, but they still fall under the medical model rather than the social model described above.

Nursing homes participating in Medicare or Medicaid are strictly regulated by the federal government, and states may have even tougher laws. Here is a website where you can check the federal and state regulations for your state:

http://www.nursinghomealert.com/federal-nursing-home-regulations-and-state-laws

To help consumers compare nursing homes, the Centers for Medicare and Medicare Services (CMS.gov) created a five-star rating system. A nursing home with a five-star rating will have much higher quality than a one-star

home. CMS.gov provides a list of nursing homes by zip code and ratings for those homes at:
  https://www.medicare.gov/nursinghomecompare/search.html

There is also a wealth of information on the Medicare website about nursing homes including this checklist for evaluating them and evaluation ratings of each Medicare-licensed facility. Note that not all nursing homes are Medicare licensed.
  https://www.medicare.gov/NursingHomeCompare/checklist.pdf

Here is another checklist for evaluating a nursing home:
  http://www.carepathways.com/checklist-nh.cfm

Paying for nursing home care

Medicare does not pay for custodial care in a nursing home. If you were admitted to a hospital for three days or more, then discharged to a skilled nursing facility for rehabilitation services or sub-acute care, Medicare currently pays on average for 10-15 days in that facility. To be eligible for this Medicare coverage, you must require skilled nursing services, and not just custodial care, and those three days as an admitted patient are critical. If you were held in the emergency room or 'for observation,' it does not count as part of those three days. You must have been admitted to the hospital.

The payment alternatives for custodial care in a nursing home are either private pay or long-term care insurance. The Veterans Administration also provides some assistance to qualified veterans. Medicaid-approved nursing homes have a certain number of beds allocated for Medicaid-eligible patients. However, many nursing homes require that new patients have sufficient resources to pay privately for a period of time before they can move to Medicaid coverage. Thus, if the individual has 'spent down' assets in an assisted living facility, he or she will not qualify for a nursing home admission in that facility.

Here are two websites that can give you an idea of what the cost of a nursing home or other care alternative is in your area:

http://www.aplaceformom.com/senior-living-cost-planner

http://longtermcare.gov/costs-how-to-pay/costs-of-care-in-your-state/

Green House Project

The Green House Project is the brainchild of Bill Thomas, a geriatrician, who envisioned a more home like environment for those in nursing home care. He designed the Green House concept to get away from the institutional atmosphere of the traditional nursing home. Residents (called 'elders') live in a specially-built home of 10-12 people, each with his or her own room and bath, with shared common spaces, creating a warm, family- and home-like atmosphere. Each home has its own dedicated staff who get to know their elders well and can engage with them and cater to their preferences. Each home also has its own open kitchen, which allows residents to eat when they want, and request food of their choice. They eat around a common table which encourages social interaction. Elders also have a say in the activities that are offered. At present, there are over 200 Green House homes in operation; some are free-standing units, while others are part of a more traditional nursing home facility. You can learn more about Green Houses at:

http://www.thegreenhouseproject.org/

Memory care units for dementia and Alzheimer's patients

Memory care units are separate wings or floors of the nursing home or assisted living facility that are specifically for people with dementia and Alzheimer's disease (a form of dementia). They may also be a section in a CCRC, or a stand-alone unit. There are different levels of memory care for residents with varying needs beyond dementia care, including assistance with the ADLs. Memory care units are secured to prevent the residents from wandering away, and they have higher staff levels with personnel especially trained in the care of such patients. Social programs and activities and the physical environment are designed specifically for this population.

A good resource on memory care is http://web28.streamhoster.com/apfmdev/dementia-guide.pdf

Chapter 9: Conclusion

Throughout the book, we have been considering the five big questions posted in the Prologue:
- Geography – what locations are you considering? Seashore? Mountains? Urban? Rural? What kind of climate are you looking for?
- Sociology – where are your friends, family, social networks, activities? A social support network is one of the most valuable assets you can have.
- Psychology – feelings about your home and home ownership. Is your home part of your personal identity? Are home-based activities such as gardening what give meaning to your life?
- Physiology – preparing for aging. How will you live in your home as you age? What design features should you be seeking?
- Financial – housing expenses can greatly impact your lifestyle.

As Richard Leider put it, home is the first component of the Good Life, the place where the people who love and support you are and where you can do the things that provide meaning to your life. So where is that? Only you can answer that question. However, I propose that it is where your friends and support networks are; where you find meaning; a place that makes you feel good; a place that you can afford and where you can feel safe and in control as you age. That may be the home you live in now; it may be some other place in town, in the next state, or even overseas; or it may be an RV or a senior facility near your family. I hope this book has been helpful to you in your quest.

About the Author

Carol King is a retiree living in the Princeton New Jersey area. Her anchoring activity after her first retirement was Director of the Next Step: Engaged Retirement & Encore Career program offered by the Princeton Senior Resource Center. This program was designed to help boomer generation people plan for a rewarding lifestyle in an encore career or traditional retirement. She also kept the books and the website for PSRC, and ran two opera video programs there.

Also in her retirement life portfolio were volunteer activities that included Ten Thousand Villages, a nonprofit fair-trade store, where she got her weekly happiness fix selling handicrafts from third-world countries. She is also treasurer of a local opera group, occasional coach of seniors in computer classes, helps out at a local music festival, and ran a MeetUp for opera lovers. Carol has served as a member of the Mercer County Community College Advisory Commission on Aging and as a deacon in her church.

Previously Carol was a college professor (tourism & hospitality management, organizational behavior, management and leadership), as well as a church financial administrator, hospitality industry consultant, food service manager and occasional technical writer. She has both an MBA and a PhD from New York University. Carol is a Certified Retirement Coach.

Since her second retirement – from the Princeton Senior Resource Center - she has sought ways to share what she has learned about the psychological impact of retirement. She has created one online program on Udemy.com, an introduction to lifestyle issues in retirement, and hopes to create others. She also maintains a website and blog at www.route2retirement.com. In 2014, She moved from a two-bedroom 1800 sq ft townhouse with basement and garage to a small one-bedroom condominium apartment in an independent senior housing facility in the Princeton NJ area. It was a good move, and in this book, Carol hopes to share her experience and what she learned from it with everyone who is asking themselves "Where shall I live when I retire?"

Resources

Books

Golant, Stephen M. *Aging in the Right Place.* HPP Health Professions Press, 2015.

Twohy Masson, Diane. *Your Senior Housing Options.* CreateSpace Independent Publishing Platform, North Charleston, SC (Amazon company), 2015.

Marcus, Clare Cooper. *House as a Mirror of Self: Exploring the Deeper Meaning of Home.* Nicolas-Hays, Inc. 2nd edition, 2006.

Stafford, Philip B. *Elderburbia: Aging with a Sense of Place in America.* Praeger, 2009.

Jameson, Marni. *AARP Downsizing the Family Home: What to Save, What to Let Go.* Sterling Publishing, 2015.

Baker, Beth. *With A Little Help from Our Friends: Creating Community as We Grow Older.* Vanderbilt University Press, 2014.

Links listed in this book

Chapter 2

The National Council on Aging's Economic Checkup calculator
https://calculator.benefitscheckup.org/calculators/move-or-stay-put

Senior Real Estate Specialist (SRES).
http://seniorsrealestate.com/

AARP rent or buy financial
http://www.aarp.org/money/budgeting-aving/rent_buy_home_calculator/

The Federal Trade Commission on reverse mortgages
https://www.consumer.ftc.gov/articles/0192-reverse-mortgages

National Council on Aging Benefits Checkup.
https://www.benefitscheckup.org/

Another benefits checkup is https://www.benefits.gov/

HUD links to various local home-buying programs
https://portal.hud.gov/hudportal/HUD?src=/buying/localbuying

LawDepot.com on rental agreements.
https://www.lawdepot.com/contracts/roommate-agreement

Roommate match sites:
Seniorly.com. https://www.seniorly.com/
Silvernest https://www.silvernest.com/

Chapter 3
Center for Universal Design, North Carolina State University
https://projects.ncsu.edu/ncsu/design/cud/pubs_p/docs/Home%20Modifications%20and%20Products.pdf

National Association of Home Builders CAPS – Certified Aging in Place Specialists.
http://www.nahb.org/en/find/directory-designee.aspx

NAHB checklist for aging in place renovations at
http://www.nahb.org/en/learn/designations/certified-aging-in-place-specialist/related-resources/aging-in-place-remodeling-checklist.aspx

Aging in Place   http://ageinplace.com

Eldercare.gov
http://eldercare.gov/Eldercare.NET/Public/Resources/Factsheets/Home_Modifications.aspx

National Association of Area Agencies on Aging locator. https://www.n4a.org/

Chapter 4
The Aging in Place Technology website https://www.ageinplacetech.com/

Ratings of places to retire http://www.milkeninstitute.org/publications/view/671

Full report at http://successfulaging.milkeninstitute.org/2014/best-cities-for-successful-aging-report-2014.pdf

WalletHub https://wallethub.com/edu/best-places-to-retire/6165/

AARP age-friendly communities http://www.aarp.org/livable-communities/network-age-friendly-communities/info-2014/member-list.html

The World Health Organization's Age-Friendly Cities Communities Program http://www.who.int/ageing/age-friendly-world/en/

US State Department Bureau of Consular Affairs. Passport, visa and international travel information https://travel.state.gov/content/travel/en.html Also, Smart Traveler Enrollment Program.

Register your trip with the nearest US embassy or consulate. https://step.state.gov/step/

International Living: https://internationalliving.com/ A blog with multiple writers providing information about relocating abroad.

Live and invest overseas http://www.liveandinvestoverseas.com/

https://bestplacesintheworldtoretire.com/

Voluntourism. org http://www.voluntourism.org also http://www.teacherswithoutborders.org and http://www.worldteach.org

Peace Corps http://www.peacecorps.gov/

Chapter 5
Professional Organizers NAPO National Association of Productivity and Professional Organizers.
http://www.napo.net/

National Association of Senior Move Managers.
https://www.nasmm.org/find/index.cfm
https://www.nasmm.org/education/guide_to_relocating.cfm

Chapter 6
Cohousing Association of the United States
http://www.cohousing.org/
National Shared Housing.org/program-directory
http://nationalsharedhousing.org/program-directory/

Tiny houses
http://www.investopedia.com/articles/investing/092815/tiny-house-movement-making-market-opportunities.asp

AARP CCRC checklist
http://www.aarp.org/relationships/caregiving-resource-center/info-09-2010/ho_what_to_ask_retirement_communities.2.html

AARP directory senior housing
http://search.seniorliving.aarp.org/

CARF, The Commission on Accreditation of Rehabilitation Facilities
http://www.carf.org/Resources/ConsumerResources/

Chapter 7
Village to Village Network http://vtvnetwork.org/

Area Agencies on Aging https://www.n4a.org/

Eldercare Locator
http://www.eldercare.gov/Eldercare.NET/Public/Index.aspx

Aging Life Care – Geriatric care managers
https://www.aginglifecare.org

Federal Wage and Hour Fact Sheets 79 B and 79A
https://www.dol.gov/whd/regs/compliance/whdfs79b.htm
and
https://www.dol.gov/whd/regs/compliance/whdfs79a.htm

Medicare-certified home health aide agencies.
https://www.medicare.gov/homehealthcompare/search.html

The Family Caregiver Alliance www.caregiver.org and
https://www.caregiver.org/hiring-home-help

Medicare check list https://www.medicare.gov/what-medicare-covers/home-health-care/Home%20Health%20Agency%20Checklist.pdf

Chapter 8
Screening instruments for ADLs and IADLs
http://www.unmc.edu/media/intmed/geriatrics/reynolds/pearlcards/functionaldisability/IADLs_form.pdf

http://clas.uiowa.edu/socialwork/files/socialwork/NursingHomeResource/documents/Katz%20ADL_LawtonIADL.pdf

https://www.payingforseniorcare.com/longtermcare/activities-of-daily-living.html

AARP checklist for assisted living facilities
http://assets.aarp.org/www.aarp.org_/promotions/text/life/AssistedLivingChecklist.pdf

Nursing home regulations
http://www.nursinghomealert.com/federal-nursing-home-regulations-and-state-laws

Centers for Medicare and Medicaid Services
https://www.cms.gov/

Medicare lists and ratings of nursing homes
https://www.medicare.gov/nursinghomecompare/search.html
https://www.medicare.gov/NursingHomeCompare/checklist.pdf

CarePathways nursing home checklist
http://www.carepathways.com/checklist-nh.cfm

Nursing home costs
http://www.aplaceformom.com/senior-living-cost-planner
http://longtermcare.gov/costs-how-to-pay/costs-of-care-in-your-state/

Green House Project
http://www.thegreenhouseproject.org/

Memory Care
http://web28.streamhoster.com/apfmdev/dementia-guide.pdf

Other helpful websites
Caring.com
Aplaceformom.com
Ourparents.com
Seniorhomes.com

www.ingramcontent.com/pod-product-compliance
Lightning Source LLC
Chambersburg PA
CBHW031408040426
42444CB00005B/475